Serena Williams

Tennis Ace

By Andrew Pina

Portions of this book originally appeared in
Serena Williams by Michael V. Uschan.

LUCENT
P R E S S

Published in 2017 by
Lucent Press, an Imprint of Greenhaven Publishing, LLC
353 3rd Avenue
Suite 255
New York, NY 10010

Designer: Deanna Paternostro
Editor: Katie Kawa

Cataloging-in-Publication Data

Names: Pina, Andrew.
Title: Serena Williams: tennis ace / Andrew Pina.
Description: New York : Lucent Press, 2017. | Series: People in the news|
Includes index.
Identifiers: ISBN 9781534560277 (library bound) | ISBN 9781534560284
(ebook)
Subjects: LCSH: Williams, Serena, 1981---Juvenile literature. | Tennis
players--United States--Biography--Juvenile literature. | African American
women tennis players--Biography--Juvenile literature.
Classification: LCC GV994.W55 P56 2017 | DDC 796.342092--dc23

Printed in the United States of America

CPSIA compliance information: Batch #CW17KL: For further information contact Greenhaven Publishing LLC,
New York, New York at 1-844-317-7404.

Please visit our website, www.greenhavenpublishing.com. For a free
color catalog of all our high-quality books, call toll free 1-844-317-7404
or fax 1-844-317-7405.

Contents

Foreword

We live in a world where the latest news is always available and where it seems we have unlimited access to the lives of the people in the news. Entire television networks are devoted to news about politics, sports, and entertainment. Social media has allowed people to have an unprecedented level of interaction with celebrities. We have more information at our fingertips than ever before. However, how much do we really know about the people we see on television news programs, social media feeds, and magazine covers?

Despite the constant stream of news, the full stories behind the lives of some of the world's most newsworthy men and women are often unknown. Who was Taylor Swift before she was a pop music phenomenon? What does LeBron James do when he is not playing basketball? What inspired Elon Musk to dream as big as he does?

This series aims to answer questions like these about some of the biggest names in pop culture, sports, politics, and technology. While the subjects of this series come from all walks of life and areas of expertise, they share a common magnetism that has made them all captivating figures in the public eye. They have shaped the world in some unique way, and—in many cases—they are poised to continue to shape the world for many years to come.

These biographies are not just a collection of basic facts. They tell compelling stories that show how each figure grew to become a powerful public personality. Each book aims to paint a complete, realistic picture of its subject—from the challenges they overcame to the controversies they caused. In doing so, each book reinforces the idea that even the most famous faces on the news are real people who are much more complex than we are often shown in brief video clips or sound bites. Readers are also reminded that there is even more to a person than what they present to the world through social media posts, press releases, and interviews. The whole story of a person's life can only be discovered by digging beneath the surface of their public persona, and that is what this series allows readers to do.

The books in this series are filled with enlightening quotes from speeches and interviews given by the subjects, as well as quotes and anecdotes from those who know their story best: family, friends, coaches, and colleagues. All quotes are noted to provide guidance for further research. Detailed lists of additional resources are also included, as are timelines, indexes, and unique photographs. These text features come together to enhance the reading experience and encourage readers to dive deeper into the stories of these influential men and women.

Fame can be fleeting, but the subjects featured in this series have real staying power. They have fundamentally impacted their respective fields and have achieved great success through hard work and true talent. They are men and women defined by their accomplishments, and they are often seen as role models for the next generation. They have left their mark on the world in a major way, and their stories are meant to inspire readers to leave their mark, too.

Introduction

A Superstar On and Off the Court

Serena Williams is a superstar on the tennis court. In 2016, she tied the legendary Steffi Graf for the most Grand Slam (Australian Open, French Open, Wimbledon, and U.S. Open) titles, and she does not appear to be slowing down in her pursuit of more victories. In addition to her Grand Slam wins, she has also brought home Olympic gold medals and can often be found dominating the doubles game alongside her older sister Venus, who is a superstar in her own right.

However, the tennis court is not the only place where Serena Williams has made her mark. She has used her fame to draw attention to important causes, including women's issues and the challenges affecting at-risk youth both in the United States and in other countries around the world. She donates her time and money to charitable efforts that are important to her, such as opening schools in Kenya. Tennis has been at the center of Williams's life since she was a little girl, but she understands that there is a world beyond the court and that world is one she can contribute to long after she has stopped playing the sport she loves.

In 2010, the groundbreaking female tennis player Billie Jean King wrote a tribute to Williams to honor her as one of *TIME* magazine's "100 Most Influential People." King stated,

Serena Williams is one of those rare champions who have transcended sports and impacted our society. In tennis, she is

Serena Williams is one of the most famous athletes in the world today.

as focused [in 2010] as she has ever been at any point in her career …

[but she is also] committed to making a difference in the lives of others. Her work with children in Kenya and here in the U.S. stresses the importance of education.

Through her charitable efforts, people are seeing her in a larger context.[1]

King was known as a pioneer in the world of women's sports, and Williams is also a pioneer in many ways. Her desire to be considered one of the greatest tennis players regardless of gender forces people to examine their biases when it comes to female athletes. Also, her daring, colorful clothing choices on the court have brought a new style to the sometimes rigid world of tennis. Finally, and perhaps most importantly, Williams has helped pave the way for other African American women in tennis. Her success—coupled with the success of her sister—has helped break down barriers in a sport that has been predominantly played by white athletes. Serena Williams has changed the sport of tennis forever, and in the process, she has become one of the most famous athletes—male or female, black or white—in the world.

Breaking Racial Barriers

When Richard Williams began teaching his daughters Venus and Serena how to play tennis as young children in Compton, California, the girls were a rarity because so few African Americans played the sport. Because of that, the sisters were sometimes ridiculed by white players with whom they shared local public tennis courts. The hurtful, racist language the girls first experienced as children did not stop as they got older. In fact, it has continued throughout their careers. Serena especially has been the victim of intense criticism throughout her career, and much of that criticism stems from her not fitting the mold of a traditional tennis player. Despite her incredible success, she has had to face harsh treatment, cruel words, body shaming, and even potential discrimination on the court. As Claudia Rankine wrote in the *New York Times*,

> *Imagine you have won 21 Grand Slam singles titles, with only four losses in your 25 appearances in the finals. Imagine that you've achieved two "Serena Slams" (four consecutive Slams in a row) ... Imagine that you're the player [tennis great] John McEnroe recently described as "the greatest player, I think, that ever lived." Imagine that, despite all this, there were so many bad calls against you, you were given as one reason video replay needed to be used on the courts. Imagine that you have to contend with critiques of your body that perpetuate racist notions that black women are hypermasculine and unattractive. Imagine being asked to comment at a news conference*

before a tournament because the president of the Russian Tennis Federation, Shamil Tarpischev, has described you and your sister as "brothers" who are "scary" to look at. Imagine.[2]

Despite the sometimes difficult path she has had to walk, Williams never gave up. She understands that she has an important place in history and can serve as a role model for other black girls who want to play this sport and are looking to see someone like them succeed. Before the Williams sisters began dominating the professional tennis circuit, only two black tennis players—Althea Gibson and Arthur Ashe—had ever won Grand Slam titles. In 1999, when Serena won the U.S. Open—her first Grand Slam title—at the age of 17, she was the first black woman to claim a Grand Slam title since Gibson won the U.S. Open in 1958, and she was the first black person to win one since Ashe won Wimbledon in 1975.

Although Williams is known for her groundbreaking accomplishments as a tennis player, breaking racial barriers in tennis—and even playing the sport itself—has been only one part of Serena's life. She has never been content to be only a tennis player.

"More to Me Than Just Tennis"

Many famous athletes are known only for what they accomplish in their chosen sports. A handful of stars, however, have such wide-ranging interests that they have become successful in other aspects of their lives. Williams's work in designing her own line of clothing, her appearances on television, and her charity work have all helped her create an identity beyond tennis. In 2008, a reporter asked her, "Why is it not enough for you to be the best tennis player in the world?" This is how she answered: "Because there is so much more to me than just tennis ... I'm a designer. I'm a thinker. I like to write. I like to do a lot of different things. While I'm

Serena's interest in fashion design began with her designing her own clothes to wear during her tennis matches.

doing all this stuff, I can still be a great tennis player."[3] Serena Williams became famous for her success on the tennis court, but she is much more than just a tennis player.

Chapter One

All in the Tennis Family

Serena Williams's life and career has been shaped in many ways by her family. Her father, Richard Williams, was the driving force behind her professional tennis career, molding her and Venus into the tennis superstars they are today. He was their coach and a familiar face in the stands during their matches, along with their mother, Oracene Price, until his health began to fail him. In 2016, he suffered a stroke but was released from the hospital, although it was reported that he did suffer some memory loss.

Serena has been open about her love for her father and her appreciation for what he did to help her and her sister become the athletes they are today. In 2009, Serena published her autobiography, *On the Line*. When the book

Richard Williams believed tennis could be the key to a better life for his daughters, and he was right.

was published, she used the dedication to honor her father for all that he had done for her: "This book is dedicated to my daddy. Your vision and undying dedication made everything possible. I love you."[4]

Serena's Parents: Richard and Oracene

Richard Williams was born in 1942 in Cedar Grove, a predominantly black section of Shreveport, Louisiana. Julia Mae Williams, his mother, raised him and his sisters alone after his father abandoned the family. Julia worked hard to support her children, but life was difficult for the family because she did not make much money and because of the racism that existed in the South at that time.

Richard moved around the country before eventually settling

Richard and Oracene got married the same year Venus was born—1980. He is shown here with Venus and Serena in 1991.

Advantage, Love, and Deuce: Scoring in Tennis

Tennis scoring is complicated and has unusual terms. Players compete until one player has won two out of three sets (for women) or three out of five sets (for men). A set consists of at least six games. The winner's score in a set could range from 6-0, in which the player wins every game, to 6-4, in which the defeated opponent manages to capture four games. A player has to win a set by at least two games, so if players are tied at 5-5, they continue to play until someone wins by a score such as 7-5 or 8-6. In some competitions, only a single tiebreaker game is required to win a set, like sudden-death overtime in football.

Scoring in a single game can also seem complicated to newcomers. A player needs four points to win a single game, and the terms for the points are 15, 30, 40, and game. If one player wins the first point, the score is called 15-love, with "love" meaning 0. As in a set, a player must win a game by two points. If players are tied at 40, it is called deuce, and they have to play until someone wins by the required margin. The player who wins the first point after deuce is said to "have the advantage" because they can win the game by winning the next point. If their opponent wins the next point, the score is again deuce.

in California. African Americans enjoyed more opportunities for a better life in California because there was less racism than in the South. Richard then met and fell in love with Oracene Price, who was working as a nurse and had three daughters—Yetunde, Lyndrea, and Isha—at the time.

Richard Williams eventually came to see tennis as a way to help his stepdaughters and daughters have a better life than he had. Serena has written, "He had a tough time [as a child], but he was determined to keep his family from the same tough time."[5] Richard read books on tennis, watched instructional videos, and practiced daily with other men at a local tennis court. A good athlete who had played baseball and football while growing up in Shreveport, Williams easily developed into a solid player.

Gangs Near the Courts

Gangs were an everyday reality in Compton while Venus and Serena were growing up. Gang members sometimes fought with and shot at each other in and around the public tennis courts where Richard taught Serena and Venus to play tennis. According to ESPNW, both Serena and her father have described the dangerous and violent atmosphere in which the Williams sisters first learned to play tennis:

Serena and Venus have talked about hearing gunfire when playing on courts in Compton. "At first," Serena writes in her biography, "I just thought someone was setting off firecrackers or popping some balloons, but once I learned what the sound meant it would shake me up pretty good."

Their father tells far more harrowing tales in his 2014 memoir, "Black and White: The Way I See It."

Richard Williams writes about having to fight gang members just to play on the courts, once getting beaten up so badly that he had several broken ribs and 10 teeth knocked out from being kicked in the mouth: "To this day [I] wear my 'toothlessness' as a badge of courage." After that beating, according to the book, Richard retaliated by bringing a shotgun to the courts, which chased away the gang members briefly. He came back the next day and fought the gang leader. "I beat him for

On June 17, 1980, Richard and Oracene had their first daughter together. Venus Ebony Starr Williams was born in Lynwood, California, but not long after that, the family moved to Oracene's hometown of Saginaw, Michigan. It was there, on September 26, 1981, that Serena Jameka Williams was born. Less than two years later, in April 1983, the family returned

everything I was worth." Finally, the leader gave up and abandoned the court with his gang.

"It had taken two years and almost destroyed my body and my spirit," Richard writes of the gang battles. "But in that moment, none of that mattered. What mattered was the courts were ours."[1]

1. Jim Caple, "Back in Compton, 'They Love Their Venus and Serena,'" ESPNW, August 28, 2015. www.espn.com/espnw/news-commentary/article/13524355/back-compton-love-their-venus-serena.

Life was not easy for kids growing up in Compton, including Venus and Serena.

to California and settled in Compton, a city near Los Angeles, which was known for its high crime rate. It was in Compton, however, that Richard's tennis dream for his family would finally begin to become a reality.

Following in Venus's Footsteps

When Venus was four years old, Richard began taking her to a nearby tennis court and teaching her to play the game he believed was his daughter's golden opportunity for fame and fortune. Three-year-old Serena accompanied her older sister to those lessons and soon began trying to play herself, even though she was not much bigger than the tennis racket. In fact, those tennis outings involved the entire family and not just the two girls who would grow up to make tennis history. In her autobiography, Serena wrote, "It was a total family affair. There was me, my older sister Venus, and my mom and dad, together with our older sisters … The older girls had been playing for a time, while I had been trudging along [to watch them]."[6]

It was not long before little Serena herself had a chance to begin playing. After begging her dad constantly, he finally handed her a racket and began tossing balls at her softly until she managed to hit a few of them. Serena at first missed most of the balls, but her dad kept encouraging her.

Over time, it became clear that Venus and Serena had the most interest in and skill at playing tennis. As they got older, Richard made the girls practice several hours almost every day of the week, sometimes requiring them to return 500 or more balls that he hit at them. He also made the girls do other drills to learn the different strokes they needed to play tennis. Despite the grueling nature of the workouts, Serena has explained that she and her sister enjoyed them because the girls knew that the drills would help make them better players: "Venus and I worked hard toward our goal from the very beginning. Dad and mom would load us, our racquets, a broom, and a bunch of milk crates filled with old tennis balls

Shown here from left to right are Lyndrea Price, Venus Williams, Oracene Price, Isha Price, and Serena Williams.

into our old red and white Volkswagen van, and we'd head off to practice tennis."[7]

The Williams family practiced on courts at a nearby public park. Unlike the pristine courts on which most youngsters their age played, the asphalt surfaces in Compton were in poor shape and had grass growing through small cracks. The courts were sometimes littered with broken glass and drug paraphernalia that the girls had to sweep away before they could play. In 1991, Richard told a reporter about the dangers he and his daughters had faced to learn tennis: "We play in hell. We've been shot at on the tennis court. But now gang members know us and protect us when the shooting starts."[8] Richard said gang members began doing that after he explained to them that he was trying to do something positive for his daughters.

Oracene and her older daughters often tagged along to watch Venus and Serena and retrieve balls during the practice sessions so they could hit them. It was only natural that they did that—the Williams family did almost everything together.

Family and Faith

Growing up as the youngest in the house, Serena had a group of older sisters who played with her and took care of her. She has written that her sisters all played important but different roles in her childhood: "Tunde was the forgiver; she had a heart of gold. Isha was the caretaker; she looked after each of us. Lyn was our play pal … Venus was my protector … on constant lookout for any situation that might cause me trouble or distress. And me, I was the princess; I was everyone's pet."[9]

Even though Richard was grooming Serena and Venus as tennis stars, he and Oracene still made them study hard. Their parents demanded they get good grades in school, and if they failed to do that, they could not practice tennis, which they loved. The sisters also had to do household chores such as clearing dinner dishes and cleaning the house. Attending church was another requirement. Oracene was a Jehovah's Witness, and all her daughters adopted her faith. This Christian sect has strict rules about behavior, including not celebrating birthdays and religious holidays, and it endorses a literal interpretation of the Bible. Serena's faith continues to be very important to her, and she credits it with helping her during periods of success and struggle in her career.

Stars Out of Nowhere

Because their father trained Venus and Serena on the nearly deserted Compton courts, few people realized how good they were becoming. That changed when he started having them compete in tournaments for young players. Venus began playing in these tournaments at age nine. To the surprise of people who were thought to be knowledgeable about California tennis, a tall, skinny, young black girl whom they had never heard of nor seen play began beating everyone. From the age of nine to eleven, Venus was undefeated in 63 matches, often playing against older players.

Serena was proud of her big sister but longed to compete herself, and she kept begging her father to let her play in a tournament. She became so frustrated that she secretly entered a tournament Venus was going to play in. When Serena's name was called to compete on the day of the tournament, her dad was shocked because he had not known she had entered it. However, Richard let her play, and she won the match. "Meeka!" he said, using his nickname for her (which was based on her middle name). "Look at you! You won! You played great!"[10] To

Serena (left) and Venus (right) began attracting national attention for their tennis talents at a young age.

Richard Faces Criticism

Richard's statements about how successful his daughters would be upset some people because bragging was not a common occurrence in tennis—especially women's tennis. Also, when newspaper and magazine stories explained how he had single-handedly molded his daughters into tennis players, some people criticized him for forcing Venus and Serena to play tennis. However, Serena argued that she never felt her father had pushed them into tennis against their will, and as an adult, she defended him against such criticism. She stated that Richard did not have to force his daughters to play tennis, because she and her sister loved the game.

her dad's amazement, Serena kept beating older players and made it to the final match. Unfortunately, her opponent was her sister Venus, who easily defeated her in the first of many times the two sisters would face off on opposite sides of the court. Even though Serena lost to Venus, she was happy just to have competed. She was also excited because of the attention she got from spectators who flocked to see the newcomer.

Although Serena was not as invincible as Venus, she lost only three matches over the next few years. When a reporter asked Serena what she enjoyed most about playing, she fired back, "Winning. I like going out and beating up on people. I get joy out of that. I really do."[11]

Bold statements such as that one set Serena apart from other players, who generally adopted a more humble attitude. Their father was even bolder in talking about his talented daughters and predicted they would become the game's best players. Most people thought his predictions sounded more like fantasy than reality because Venus and Serena were striving for success in a sport in which very few African Americans had become stars.

Richard's predictions began to come true in 1990 when 10-year-old Venus won the Southern California championships for girls 10 and younger. Because California has so many talented players, the victory brought her national fame. Venus, just a fifth-grade student, was even featured on the front page of the famous *New York Times* newspaper in a story that also mentioned her talented younger sister.

Chapter Two

Training for the Pros

As Venus and Serena began to grow up and grow into talented young tennis players, Richard Williams found himself at a crossroads. He loved teaching his daughters and helping them grow into the best players they could be, but it became clear that they needed more than he could provide. The skills of the students were quickly surpassing the skills of their teacher. In an interview with *Sports Illustrated* magazine for a 1991 story about Venus, Richard admitted, "Her skills have already passed me ... I need someone to give her better practice and take her to the next level."[12]

Richard found what he was looking for—a tennis academy where many of the nation's top young talents sharpened their skills. However, it was located on the other side of the country.

Venus is shown here at the Rick Macci Tennis Academy, where both she and Serena trained to become even better athletes.

Despite the distance, Richard knew this was the right decision, and he moved the family to Florida so Venus and Serena could train at the Rick Macci Tennis Academy.

This move was meant to help both sisters grow as tennis players. Although Venus was the more famous and more successful sister at the time, Richard knew Serena was something special, too. In fact, when Rick Macci told Richard, "It looks like you have the next Michael Jordan on your hands," Richard replied, "No, Mr. Macci, we've got the next two Michael Jordans."[13]

Having a "Normal Life"

When Richard moved his family to Florida, he made a decision that astounded some people in the tennis world: He decided his daughters would no longer compete in junior tournaments. He did not like the atmosphere at the tournaments because so many parents pushed their children in extreme ways and said hurtful things—including racist remarks—about Venus and Serena.

Years later, Serena said that her father made the right decision for his daughters:

He didn't like the way parents and coaches were all over their junior players … He wanted us to have a normal life. He didn't want to be one of those parents pushing and pushing his kids down a path they might not necessarily have chosen for themselves. Plus, he thought we could get better competition, just hitting with these pros and coaches and working on our fundamentals.

I've always thought this was a genius move.[14]

The normal life Richard wanted for Venus and Serena included going to school; he and Oracene continued to demand that they work hard in their classes, even though they would also be training hard. By not competing in tournaments, which required extensive travel, they would have more time to study, pursue other interests, and have time with their family.

Training Time

Macci shared responsibility for the sisters' overall development with their father, who continued to help teach his daughters on a daily basis. The sisters also worked with Dave Rineberg, a hitting coach who taught them how to perform various shots. He also practiced against the girls to get them accustomed to playing a superior opponent.

During this period, Venus was the unrivaled star. Even though Venus received more direct training from coaches at that time, Serena was not jealous of the attention her older sister got. One reason is that Richard was working with Serena more, and she enjoyed the extra time she was able to spend learning the game from her father. Serena said, "For me, that was one of the great benefits of being on the second string, in terms of everyone's expectations: I finally had my dad to myself."[15]

Preparing for Professional Careers

Venus and Serena practiced tennis five or six hours daily, six days a week. In 1993, Richard and Oracene took control of their education and began homeschooling Venus and Serena. Macci said that, even though Richard always pushed his daughters hard in practice, he sometimes put their need to study ahead of learning how to play: "[He's] always been an incredible father to those two girls ... I can remember 50 times when he called off practice because Venus's grades were

Meeting Venus
and Serena

In December 1992, Dave Rineberg became the hitting coach for Venus and Serena Williams, a position he held for seven years. He taught them how to hit shots and played against them to teach them on-court strategy. In his book about his experience with the Williams sisters, Rineberg described the first time he met them. He said he was not only impressed by the intensity with which they played, but also by how polite they were when their father Richard introduced them to him. Rineberg wrote that Venus introduced herself first, and then her younger sister, who seemed more shy, followed:

> *"Hi, I am Venus. It is nice to meet you." I noticed the politeness. What a welcome change. I was teaching about eight hours of junior tennis a week and only a few of my students had such good manners ... "Hi, I am Serena." She was polite also, but her physique was smaller [than her sister's] and more solid. She seemed to shy away quickly. Maybe she was just stepping back into Venus's shadow where she felt more comfortable ... Both girls kissed their father and then started slapping the ball back and forth, as if they were in a third set of the U.S. Open finals.*[1]

1. Dave Rineberg, *Venus & Serena: My Seven Years as Hitting Coach for the Williams Sisters.* Hollywood, FL: Frederick Fell, 2001, pp. 17–18.

down. They'd be in my office studying French, and I'd be saying, 'Hey, we've got to work.'"[16]

Because Venus and Serena were so busy studying and playing tennis, their parents limited their free time. They could not watch much television, they did not go to parties, and they had an early bedtime every night. Their lives were not all hard work, though. Rineberg remembers that Richard always tried to make

Serena Williams and Billie Jean King played together when Serena was a young girl. Now, they are considered two of the most famous figures in the history of women's tennis.

practice enjoyable for his daughters so they would not get bored. Rineberg also said Richard sometimes canceled practice and took his daughters to nearby Walt Disney World so they could relax. As Macci said, "He was good at keeping it fun for them. He used to say that he believed it was family first, then education, then religion, and then maybe tennis. The bottom line was, Richard was going to be a parent first and his coaching and managing would all be second."[17]

Although Richard did not want his daughters competing on the junior circuit, he occasionally allowed them to play publicly in special events. One was the Family Circle Magazine Cup at Hilton Head, South Carolina, a professional event famed for showcasing young stars. On April 5, 1992, 10-year-old Serena teamed with Billie Jean King to play 11-year-old Venus and ex-pro Rosie Casals in an exhibition doubles match.

Serena and Billie Jean King won the match. Afterward, King expressed her amazement at how good the sisters were at such a young age: "I don't think I even knew what tennis was at that age, but the important thing is that they go slowly and do the right thing. That's what makes champions."[18]

Richard wanted his daughters to move slowly in preparing for their professional careers. The problem was that the huge potential Venus and Serena had made it hard for them to remain amateurs.

Potential Fame and Fortune

The news media kept writing stories about Venus and Serena even though they were not competing in junior tournaments. Media interest was fueled not only by the talent the sisters had already displayed at such a young age, but also by the fact that they were African Americans in a mostly white sport.

The fame the news coverage brought them and their vast potential for future success also captured the attention of professional sports agents, who believed the sisters could earn huge amounts of money by endorsing products such as tennis equipment. The agents wanted to represent them because they would receive a percentage of any business deals they arranged for their clients—and the girls' earning potential was huge.

Most of the attention was focused on Venus, who developed more quickly than her younger sister. When Venus was only 10 years old, top sports agents were already trying to persuade her dad to sign a contract. Richard said agents were promising him homes, cars, and millions of dollars if Venus signed with them. Although Richard admitted it would be nice to have so much money, he said he would not sign deals because he worried they could hurt Venus.

Venus, however, was already planning to play professionally. In November 1993, when she was 13 years old, a *New York Times* story described her as a bright eighth-grader who was studying French and Spanish because they were languages she could use when she played professional tournaments in

Venus developed as a tennis player more quickly than Serena did, which is why agents first took notice only of her.

Europe. Venus also explained her own timetable for the future: "I want to turn pro when I'm 15. I don't want to go too early or too late."[19]

However, a rules change by the Women's Tennis Association (WTA), the governing body for professional women's tennis, would speed up Venus's debut as a professional player.

Venus Goes Pro

In 1994, the Women's Tennis Association raised the age women could turn professional. The WTA ruled that, starting in 1995, the minimum age for a professional would be 15—one year older than it had been previously—and that minimum age would keep rising annually until it hit 18. The rule also limited the number of tournaments younger players could play each year until they turned 18. The WTA raised the age because some young players had encountered problems dealing with the pro lifestyle. The WTA, however, had a clause that allowed players who were close to becoming 14 to turn professional earlier. Because Venus would turn 14 on June 17, 1994, it was decided that she would turn pro to beat the new age restrictions. The family chose the Bank of the West Classic in Oakland, California, for her

Venus is shown here making her professional tennis debut in 1994.

professional debut.

Venus had not played a competitive match for several years, but on October 31, she defeated Shaun Stafford in straight sets. In the second round, Venus faced Arantxa Sánchez Vicario, the world's top-ranked female tennis player. Although Venus won the first set, her opponent battled back to take the next two sets and win the match.

Serena's Time in the Spotlight

Serena was excited for Venus and even traveled to California to be her sister's hitting partner, helping Venus prepare for the competition. When reporters asked Richard questions about Venus, he was happy to answer them all, but he also asked them, "Have you

After Venus's career took off, Serena, shown here with her father, began planning for her own professional career.

Serena's Reaction

In her autobiography, Serena Williams described how thrilled she was when Venus played her first professional match on October 31, 1994:

> I remember it as such an exciting moment, such an exciting time. We didn't have enough money for all of us to travel from Florida, but I went as Venus's hitting partner. Lyn came, too. What a thrill! To be down on those courts with all those great players! Oh my goodness, I was so pumped! Daddy told me to hit as hard as I could when I was working with Venus, and I imagined that I was playing in the tournament and that Venus was the top seed and that all these people were watching us and cheering for us ... I can't even tell you how happy I was for V [when she won her first match]. I was over the moon and back again. It was crazy! The win earned Venus a whopping $5,350 in prize money —which was just about a fortune to her at the time. Daddy's idea was to let us keep all the money we earned, and to learn to be responsible for it right away, so Venus started to look really, really rich in my eyes, and I was only too happy to let her spoil me.[1]

1. Serena Williams with Daniel Paisner, *On the Line*. Boston, MA: Grand Central, 2009, pp. 111-112.

seen my other daughter Serena play? She's better than Venus."[20] It would not be long before Serena would make her own professional debut to show the world what she could do.

Chapter Three

From the Sidelines to the Court

As Venus Williams embarked on her professional career, things initially did not change much for Serena. She wanted to be a pro every bit as much as her older sister, but she had to wait. In her autobiography, Serena noted, "I wanted to be out there playing, making noise of my own. I wanted what Venus had and I didn't want to wait for it to be my turn. I wanted it right away."[21] As it turned out, Serena did not have to wait long to get her wish.

When Serena turned 14 on September 26, 1995, she was faced with two options when it came to her professional career: She either had to turn pro before the end of the year, or she was going to have to wait until she was 16, playing a restricted number of games until her 18th birthday. Serena wanted to finally move from the sidelines, watching her sister play professional tennis, to the professional court. She made the decision to begin playing professionally at 14 years old, and her family supported her just as they had supported Venus's decision to do the same thing.

In October 1995, Serena made her professional debut at the Bell Challenge in Quebec City, Canada. Unlike Venus, Serena did not taste success her first time playing as a pro. She lost to 18-year-old Annie Miller 6–1, 6–1. The entire match took less than an hour.

Serena did not give up after that first loss, though. She continued to train and work hard to make a name for herself as a professional player just like her sister. It took Serena a little longer than Venus to begin her rise to superstardom, but her journey to professional success helped mold her into the competitive, driven player she is known as today.

A Breakthrough Year

Richard and Oracene Williams had spent more than a decade grooming their daughters for professional tennis careers. However, after their daughters made it to the pros, both parents expressed doubts about the girls turning pro at such a young age. Richard was especially concerned about Serena. In a 1995 interview with the *New York Times*, he said, "I'm just afraid, especially with Serena, who's a perfectionist, that she'll take it so seriously that she'll never have fun with it, be a flop at 18."[22] To make sure their daughters did not lose interest in tennis or develop personal problems like some teens who had turned pro early, Oracene and Richard limited the girls' playing schedules for

Serena is shown here in 1997, which was a breakthrough year for both Williams sisters.

the next few years.

In 1996, Venus played without much success in five tournaments, and Serena did not play professionally at all as she concentrated on improving enough to be competitive as a professional. Then, in 1997, the sisters began to show the talent that had led Richard to boast that each of his daughters could one day become the world's best player.

In October, at the Ameritech Cup in Chicago, Serena defeated Monica Seles and Mary Pierce. She made history at the time as the lowest-ranked player to record her first career wins over two players in the top 10 in the world rankings. Seles was the world's number 4 player and Pierce was number 7. Although Serena lost to Lindsay Davenport in the semifinals, it was a fantastic performance for a 16-year-old. It was also one that allowed her to emerge from her sister's shadow as a good player in her own right.

Venus's own breakthrough season was highlighted by her sensational run to the title match of the U.S. Open, one of the four annual Grand Slam events that are the most important in tennis. However, Martina Hingis, another teenage star, defeated her 6–0, 6–4 for the title. That loss was actually not Venus's most publicized match. Her semifinal win over Romanian player Irina Spirlea generated a firestorm of controversy, including charges of racism by Richard Williams. The incident also made public the problems the two sisters had experienced in getting along with other players.

Problems Made Public

The 1997 U.S. Open was played in a new stadium named after Arthur Ashe and began on the 70th birthday of Althea Gibson. What was meant to be a celebration of the two most successful African American players in tennis history was tainted by discussions of whether or not racism was still a major factor in the sport. In the semifinal match, Irina Spirlea intentionally collided with Venus while they were changing sides of the court between games. Richard Williams claimed Spirlea's action was racially

The 1997 U.S. Open was a huge moment for Venus, but it also highlighted the struggles the Williams sisters faced as successful African American women in a sport dominated by white players.

motivated, but Spirlea said afterward that she did it because she believed Venus was acting haughty, partly because of all the media attention she got as a rising African American star in a sport that was still mostly played by white men and women.

After Venus lost to Hingis in the title match, the news media questioned her about her dad's claim of racism. Venus tried to evade the question. She answered that, since the tournament was supposed to have been about racial harmony, "I think this is definitely ruining the mood, these questions about racism."[23] When reporters continued asking her about the issue, she left the interview session.

Although some players may have harbored racist attitudes toward Venus and Serena, some observers claimed racism was not the main reason why Venus and Serena were having trouble being accepted by other players. One problem they faced in making friends was the jealousy other players had over their swift rise to fame and fortune. In 1995, when Annie Miller defeated Serena in her pro debut, Miller had sarcastically commented, "I guess I played a celebrity."[24] The remark showed how much players resented the mass media attention Venus and Serena had been receiving. Their fame also helped them secure huge endorsement contracts that most other players could only dream about, and that made other players even more envious of the sisters. In May 1995, Reebok signed Venus to an endorsement contract worth $12 million, and in January 1998, Serena landed a similar deal with Puma.

Others argued that it was the sisters' attitude that made them outsiders in the tennis world. During the 1997 U.S. Open, it was written of Venus that "[p]layers complained publicly about her arrogance, her unfriendly demeanor, her trash-talking."[25] However, many sports reporters have noted that great competitors are often not known for being friendly with those they play against. Venus and Serena were no different from other focused, competitive greats in the world of sports.

Racist Attitudes Remain

In a 2003 article for *The Guardian*, Martin Jacques wrote about how racist attitudes have followed Serena and Venus Williams throughout their careers:

> *As race courses through the veins of tennis, people pretend it doesn't exist. Instead the Williams sisters, together with their father, are subjected to a steady stream of criticism, denigration, accusation and innuendo: their physique is somehow an unfair advantage (those of Afro descent are built differently), they are arrogant and aloof (they are proud and self-confident), they are not popular with the other players (they come from a very different culture and, let us not forget, there is plenty of evidence of racism among their colleagues ...)*[1]

Today, the racist attitudes toward the sisters can often be seen on social media, and much of it is especially directed toward Serena, as she is the sister most

Their unfriendly attitude toward competitors did not extend to each other. When they met as professionals for the first time in January 1998, Venus defeated Serena at the Australian Open. Afterward, Venus was overheard telling her sister, "I'm sorry I had to take you out, Serena."[26] However, they continued battling other players and occasionally each other to pursue their dreams of becoming the highest-ranked players in the world. In the process, they began making tennis history.

Sisters Making History

On March 1, 1999, Serena defeated Amelie Mauresmo 6–2, 3–6, 7–6 to win her first tournament, the Gaz de France in Paris. Just a few hours later and several thousand miles away, Venus won

often in the spotlight in recent years. In an article—titled "Serena Williams Is Constantly the Target of Disgusting Racist and Sexist Attacks"—for the online news outlet Vox, Jenée Desmond-Harris reported,

> All too often, instead of being celebrated, [Serena is] targeted with outrageous racist and sexist comments.
>
> For example, in the moments surrounding her win at the French Open in June 2015, Williams was compared to an animal, likened to a man, and deemed frightening and horrifyingly unattractive. One Twitter user wrote that Williams "looks like a gorilla, and sounds like a gorilla when she grunts while hitting the ball. In conclusion, she is a gorilla." And another described her as "so unbelievably dominant ... and manly."[2]

1. Martin Jacques, "Tennis Is Racist—It's Time We Did Something About It," *The Guardian*, June 25, 2003. www.theguardian.com/sport/2003/jun/25/wimbledon2003.tennis11.

2. Jenée Desmond-Harris, "Serena Williams Is Constantly the Target of Disgusting Racist and Sexist Attacks," Vox, September 7, 2016. www.vox.com/2015/3/11/8189679/serena-williams-indian-wells-racism.

the IGA Superthrift Classic in Oklahoma City, Oklahoma. The twin wins made them the first sisters to win tournaments on the same day. The victory was Venus's fourth tournament title. Although Serena's tournament win was only her first, she had the satisfaction of capturing it at the age of 17 years and 5 months, which made her 3 months younger than Venus had been when she clinched her first tournament victory.

When Serena and Venus were not on the road playing in tournaments, they practiced together with their dad and other coaches. They lived together in a home they built in Florida not far from where their parents lived. After being homeschooled for several years, they both graduated from a private high school named Driftwood Academy—Venus in 1998 and Serena in 1999. After they graduated, they both began studying fashion design at the Art Institute of Florida.

The close relationship between the sisters made them natural partners in women's doubles—a format matching two players of the same sex against another duo—and enabled them to make more history. In June 1999, they won the French Open

Venus and Serena were happy to win the 1999 French Open women's doubles championship, but they both still wanted to win a Grand Slam singles title.

"The Sport's Most Marketable Faces"

The emergence of Serena Williams as a great player in 1999 helped the Williams sisters reach new heights of global fame. The November 1999 issue of *Tennis* magazine noted the star power that Venus and Serena shared:

> It's no stretch to say that tennis has seldom, if ever, seen media stars like the Williams sisters. [Even] before they rose to career-high rankings of No. 3 (Venus) and No. 4 (Serena), they'd already become the sport's most marketable faces. Together, the Williamses have made tennis an in-your-face game, and their brash comments—"I think everyone I play is intimidated by me," says Serena—have become the norm. Though much is made, and rightly so, of their being role models for other African-Americans, their appeal crosses age, gender, and racial lines. At the 1999 Lipton Championships, the Williams' trademark beaded hairstyles inspired tournament organizers to set up a booth where you could be made to look just like them—for $5 a braid. Even away from the courts, a sighting of Venus or Serena is enough to stop a taxi driver, an elderly gift shop clerk, a little girl in tennis gear, and a middle-aged couple, one of whom introduces herself as a psychic. "Other people say we're [arrogant], but we're really not," Serena says before rushing off for her one-on-one with Jay Leno. "We say it and we mean it. We know how to get what we want."[1]

1. Johnette Howard, "Bragging Rights," *Tennis*, November 1999, p. 36.

women's doubles championship by beating Martina Hingis and Anna Kournikova 6–3, 6–7, 8–6. The victory, however, was only a consolation for having failed to win the singles title. Serena showed her disappointment when she noted, "I'm sure anyone who says they would prefer to win the doubles title [instead of a singles title], they would have to be mentally unsound."[27]

Winning a Grand Slam singles title is the true mark of a great tennis player—and Venus and Serena were in a family race to be the first sister to win one.

Sibling Rivalry

During the 1999 season, Serena began to show the promise her father had predicted when he said she would be better than Venus. Although the 5-foot, 9-inch (1.75 m) Serena was 4 inches (10.16 cm) shorter than Venus, she was more muscular and could hit as powerfully as her older sister. In fact, they were both among the strongest, hardest serving, and most athletic female players the game had ever seen.

As Serena kept improving, she found that Venus was one of her toughest opponents, and in March, they met in Florida for the title in the Lipton Championships. In the first championship match between sisters since Maud Watson had defeated her sibling, Lilian, to win Wimbledon in 1884, Venus triumphed 6–1,

Venus and Serena have faced each other in many important matches, including Grand Slam finals, throughout their careers.

4–6, 6–4. Serena said she did not play well but added, "I always dreamed of seeing [Venus] on the other side of the net, and now that my game is taken to a different level, it's going to happen more."[28]

The loss dropped Serena to a lifetime record of 0–3 against Venus in pro matches, but she would finally beat her older sister in another championship matchup. In the fall, Serena defeated Venus 6–1, 3–6, 6–3 in Munich, Germany, in the Grand Slam Cup.

U.S. Open Champion

Despite the satisfaction of finally having beaten Venus, it was a title Serena won later in 1999 that was actually much more important to her. In September, she upstaged Venus by winning the U.S. Open to become the first of the two sisters to capture a Grand Slam title. At first, it looked as if the two sisters would be

Serena told reporters after her 1999 U.S. Open victory that this was the Grand Slam event she most wanted to win.

Talking to the President

Serena Williams's victory was the first in a Grand Slam by an African American in decades. The victory electrified the sports world not only because Serena was African American, but also because she was only 17. More people than usual had watched the match on television to see if Serena could make history. Among them was the president of the United States. During her post-match news conference, President Bill Clinton called Serena. The conversation was detailed in *Tennis* magazine:

> *President Clinton: "Congratulations. We're proud of you. Tell your family I want y'all to come to the White House. You have a lot of fans there."*
>
> *Serena: "Really?"*
>
> *President Clinton: "We were thrilled. I mean, the whole White House was out there cheering for you."*
>
> *Serena: "Wow, I'm so excited. We're definitely going to make a trip."[1]*

1. Stephen Tignor, "Made in America," *Tennis*, November 1999, p. 85.

facing each other for the title as they breezed through the early rounds of play. However, when Venus lost a dramatic semifinal match to Martina Hingis, Serena wound up facing the woman who beat her sister for the title.

On September 12, just two weeks before her 18th birthday, Serena upset Hingis 6–3, 7–6 to become one of the youngest champions in U.S. Open history. When Serena finally ended the match, a rowdy crowd of 22,000 fans erupted with screams of joy over her victory, and so did Serena. Afterward, she told reporters she was so excited she did not know what to do when she won: "'Should I scream, should I yell or should I cry?' And I guess I ended up doing them all."[29]

Serena added to her dramatic win the next day by teaming with Venus to win the women's doubles title as they defeated Chanda Rubin and Sandrine Testud 4–6, 6–1, 6–4. Serena said she played hard to make sure her sister also got a title, saying, "I don't want to let Venus down at all."[30] Although Venus and Serena shared that doubles title, the 1999 U.S. Open was the tournament in which Serena finally surpassed her sister's accomplishments as a singles player.

Chapter Four

Four in a Row:
The Serena Slam

Serena's victory in the 1999 U.S. Open marked the start of a new chapter in the history of women's tennis—a chapter in which she and her sister were the undisputed main characters. As the 21st century began, it was hard to find a Grand Slam final that did not feature one or both sisters.

Venus and Serena were on top of the tennis world in the early 2000s, but it was Serena who accomplished something so rare that the feat was named after her: the Serena Slam. She was excited to win one Grand Slam final in 1999, but just a few years later, she won four in a row.

Venus Reaches the Top

It was reported that Venus was unhappy to lose to her little sister, but Serena believed everything was going according to plan: "I was always the one who said, 'I want to win the US Open,' and Venus, she always wanted Wimbledon."[31] Venus's dream came true in July 2000 when she won Wimbledon. However, the joy Venus felt in capturing her favorite Grand Slam tournament was dimmed slightly by the fact that she had to beat Serena in a semifinal match to do it. After the 6–2, 7–6 victory, Venus admitted,

I'm always the big sister … I always take care of Serena, no

matter what. I always make the decisions. I'm always a role model for Serena. I'm the big sister. I always worry about her. It's really bitter. But someone had to move on. It was either going to be me or Serena. In this instance, it was me.[32]

The day after beating Serena, Venus defeated defending champion Lindsay Davenport 6–3, 7–6 to become only the second black woman after Althea Gibson to win the sport's most prestigious tournament. Just two days later, Venus and Serena made more history by becoming the first sisters to win the tournament's women's doubles championship.

In September, Venus won the U.S. Open for her second Grand Slam title, giving her one more than Serena, and in 2001, she won both those tournaments again. Her victory in the 2001 U.S. Open

Serena and Venus made history in 2000 as the first sisters to win the Wimbledon women's doubles tournament.

capped off a historic match, as Venus and Serena became the first sisters to face each other for the title. After Venus defeated Serena 6–2, 6–4, she leaned across the net on the tennis court, hugged Serena, and told her she loved her.

Losing to Venus was not as devastating for Serena as falling to another opponent because the sisters always rejoiced in each other's successes. However, because Serena was a fierce competitor, the loss still bothered her. It made Serena work even harder to step up her game so she could keep pace with her older sister's accomplishments.

Both sisters had always believed they were talented enough to be the top-ranked player in the world. Tennis rankings are based on points players accumulate in tournaments, especially Grand Slam events, which award the most points to winners. Venus's string of Grand Slam victories helped her reach that goal on February 25, 2002, but she held it only until March 17, when Jennifer Capriati reclaimed the top spot.

When Serena set her mind on becoming the world's best player, she knew she had to win more Grand Slam tournaments to do it. What Serena did not know was how fast she would reach her goal and how Venus would play a major part in her rise to the number 1 ranking.

Victory on Clay

In January 2002, an ankle injury kept Serena out of the Australian Open. However, it did not keep her from participating in any other Grand Slam events that year. In fact, when Serena stepped on the court to play in the next Grand Slam tournament that year—the French Open—she was determined to show that she had improved after a stretch without any Grand Slam victories.

The French Open is played on clay, a softer surface that makes players change their game. Serena had struggled on clay in the past, but she had improved so much that she won the

The 2002 French Open was the first event in what became known as the first Serena Slam.

tournament in June 2002 to secure her second Grand Slam title. Most players who win major competitions in any sport want to win at least one more to prove that the first was not a fluke. Serena proved this by beating Venus 7–5, 6–3 in the French Open title match. Serena explained afterward why the victory was important to her: "I was really fighting for this for so long. At one point, I wouldn't get past the quarters, then I got to the [2001 U.S. Open] final, maybe a semi here and there. But it was just kind of discouraging. I didn't want to be a one-hit wonder."[33]

Winning Wimbledon

In July 2002, Wimbledon's grass courts presented another challenging surface for Serena. However, Serena's new dominance was on display once again. Her experience and her desire to achieve greatness helped her win a second straight Grand Slam event. Her 7–6, 6–3 victory in the title match once again came at the expense of her sister, who had dominated her for years.

Sports Illustrated writer L. Jon Wertheim raved about how exciting the all-Williams final had been and wrote that "it's clear that Serena has become the best player in women's tennis."[34] That was an easy statement to make because by winning Wimbledon,

Serena accumulated enough points to be ranked number 1 in the world. Venus was ranked second, which made them the first sisters to hold the top two spots in the women's tennis rankings.

Completing the Slam

The U.S. Open in September is the last of the four annual Grand Slam events. The Williams sisters showed that they deserved the top two rankings by meeting again for the title. Serena prevailed 6–4, 6–3 for her third straight Grand Slam title.

After her victory, Serena commented, "I prefer to play Venus [in a final] because that means that we have reached our maximum potential and that we'll both go home win-ners."[35] Venus, how-ever, was feeling the weight of three straight Grand Slam losses. She said she would only play a few more tournaments in 2002 before taking time off to recover from an exhausting season.

In baseball, a grand slam is a bases-loaded home run that drives in four runs. That term was transferred to ten-nis and golf to refer to what happens when someone wins the four major tournaments in each sport. When

Few tennis players have held all four major titles at the same time. Serena Williams joined their exclusive company in January 2003 after winning the Australian Open and completing the Serena Slam.

"Endure. Persevere. Stand Tall."

Serena Williams knows that it is as important to be mentally prepared to play tennis as it is to be in top physical condition. As a professional, she began writing herself notes for each match she played. They ranged from statements about God or African American history to reminders not to hit the ball so hard that it went out of bounds. Many were psychological reminders designed to motivate her to play up to her potential. This match note was shared in her autobiography:

> *Fear will hold U back. Champions fear nothing. Only fear God and give Him glory. Fear no man (woman). Use those legs. God gave them to U for a reason. Put your gifts to work. Take the ball on the rise. Attack the short ball—it's waiting for U!!! Show no emotion. U R black and U can endure anything. Endure. Persevere. Stand tall.*[1]

1. Serena Williams with Daniel Paisner, *On the Line*. Boston, MA: Grand Central, 2009, p. 122.

Serena played in the 2003 Australian Open, she had a chance to make history by capturing her fourth straight major title.

On January 25, 2003, Serena and Venus met yet again in the title match. Although Venus had worked hard to improve and was a much tougher foe than she had been in previous matches, Serena defeated her one more time in a challenging three-set match 7–6, 3–6, 6–4. She told a cheering crowd after her victory, "I never get choked up, never, but I'm really emotional right now and really, really happy. I'd like to thank my mom and dad for always supporting me."[36] Then she began to cry so hard that she could not continue talking.

Because the four victories had not come in a single year, her feat was called a Serena Slam instead of a Grand Slam.

The unusual designation was fitting because Serena was different in many ways from other players.

Facing Criticism

The most obvious way the Williams sisters differed from other players was the color of their skin. Serena and Venus occasionally encountered racism at tour events. The most shocking example of this occurred in March 2001 when Serena defeated Kim Clijsters 4–6, 6–4, 6–2 to win a tournament in Indian Wells, California. Before the final match, 15,000 fans booed Richard and Venus Williams when they took their seats to watch Serena play. Richard claimed later that some of them even shouted racial slurs at them. Richard raised his fist at those who were booing, but his gesture only made the crowd yell louder.

During the match, the crowd booed Serena while cheering loudly for Clijsters. Serena was shocked by the outbursts: "How many people do you know who would go out and jeer a 19-year-old? Come on, I'm just a kid … I'm just an innocent person."[37] Serena later claimed that racism must have motivated some of the hostile reaction she got. However, she battled on through the catcalls and boos to win the title and afterward claimed, "I won a big battle today mentally. I think a champion can come through."[38] Serena had always enjoyed that tournament, but she and Venus vowed to never play in it again because of the way the fans had treated them. Serena eventually returned to play at Indian Wells in 2015, and Venus played there again in 2016.

The hostile reception, however, was not entirely based on racism. Many fans were upset that Venus had backed out of a semifinals match against Serena just four minutes before it was to have started. Although Venus told officials she was suffering from heat exhaustion and tendonitis, some people believed Richard had forced his daughter to withdraw to ensure Serena would win the tournament for a second straight year. That theory seemed plausible to some people because of allegations that Richard had manipulated his daughters' matches in the past. One accusation claimed he had ordered Serena to play poorly against Venus in the 2000 Wimbledon semifinals so Venus could win her first Grand Slam title.

Even though Richard, Serena, and Venus all denied such allegations, the charges continued to haunt them whenever the two sisters played each other or were expected to meet in a match. In fact, the two best players in the world became magnets for criticism for almost everything they did—from skipping lesser tournaments to not being friendlier with their competitors. Venus and Serena did play fewer tournaments than most players, but that was because they wanted to pursue other interests, including taking classes on designing clothes and appearing on television shows. The sisters were also singled out for keeping their distance from other players, even though many of their competitors also remained aloof from their peers.

Serena and Venus were even criticized because they were more athletic and muscular than most female tennis players. Some people adopted the racist and sexist attitude that their bodies were unfeminine and hurt the sport. The sisters were also judged

Serena wore her trademark bright colors during her return to Indian Wells in 2015.

for the clothes they wore when they played tennis. Until Serena and Venus, players typically wore simple white skirts and tops, but the Williams sisters began to change things by wearing daring outfits and bright colors.

The volleys of criticism directed against the sisters did not bother Serena. That was because she had so much self-confidence both on and off the court. After winning Wimbledon in 2002, she told reporters,

You have to be satisfied with you and who you are. Venus and I have learned that we're satisfied and we're happy with us. We don't have any problem with anyone because you have to be happy with the person inside. When you're a little bitter and

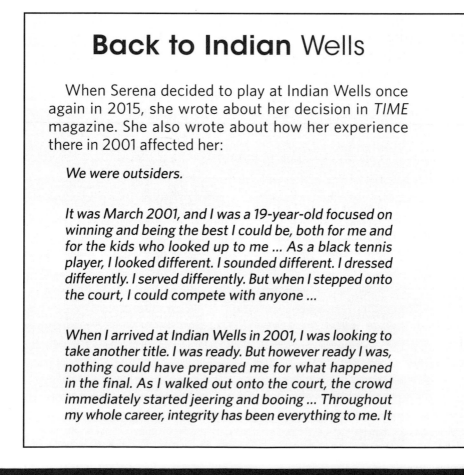

Back to Indian Wells

When Serena decided to play at Indian Wells once again in 2015, she wrote about her decision in *TIME* magazine. She also wrote about how her experience there in 2001 affected her:

We were outsiders.

It was March 2001, and I was a 19-year-old focused on winning and being the best I could be, both for me and for the kids who looked up to me ... As a black tennis player, I looked different. I sounded different. I dressed differently. I served differently. But when I stepped onto the court, I could compete with anyone ...

When I arrived at Indian Wells in 2001, I was looking to take another title. I was ready. But however ready I was, nothing could have prepared me for what happened in the final. As I walked out onto the court, the crowd immediately started jeering and booing ... Throughout my whole career, integrity has been everything to me. It a little angry, then you're going to become resentful. Instead of becoming resentful, you should go do something about it.[39]

Sisterhood Means More Than Success

Serena's positive mental attitude extended to her historic clashes with her sister, especially her four straight victories in Grand Slam events in 2002 and 2003. When Serena defeated Venus in January 2003 to complete the Serena Slam, many newspaper and magazine articles ran stories about the role reversal in which Serena had become the family's dominant

is also everything and more to Venus. The false allegations that our matches were fixed hurt, cut and ripped into us deeply. The undercurrent of racism was painful, confusing and unfair. In a game I loved with all my heart, at one of my most cherished tournaments, I suddenly felt unwelcome, alone and afraid ...

I have thought about going back to Indian Wells many times over my career. I said a few times that I would never play there again. And believe me, I meant it. I admit it scared me. What if I walked onto the court and the entire crowd booed me? The nightmare would start all over ...

I'm fortunate to be at a point in my career where I have nothing to prove. I'm still as driven as ever, but the ride is a little easier. I play for the love of the game. And it is with that love in mind, and a new understanding of the true meaning of forgiveness, that I will proudly return to Indian Wells in 2015.[1]

1. Serena Williams, "Serena Williams: I'm Going Back to Indian Wells," *TIME*, February 4, 2015. time.com/3694659/serena-williams-indian-wells/.

Bolder Fashions

Even when Serena failed to win a tournament, she was still able to make headlines and influence her sport with the bold, colorful outfits she wore while playing. Serena and Venus both competed in clothes that were more adventurous than anything ever seen before in women's tennis. As a result, they influenced the clothing styles tennis players and other athletes began wearing. Serena explained how much the sisters enjoyed doing that:

Venus and I have a lot of fun with fashion on the tennis court. When we started playing professionally we wore our hair braided with lots and lots of white beads in them. At first, the tennis world didn't know what to make of our look. Then, just when they had gotten used to it, we switched up and sported new styles. We have adopted different hairstyles ever since. We also try different fashions on the court. In the past, tennis players usually wore a lot of white and conservative styles and colors. We bring our flair to the sport by wear-

ing new and exciting shapes, designs and colors that we think flatter our looks. Just because everyone else wears certain brands and styles of clothes doesn't mean that you have to follow their lead.[1]

1. Venus and Serena Williams with Hilary Beard, *Venus & Serena: Serving from the Hip, 10 Rules for Living, Loving and Winning.* Boston, MA: Houghton Mifflin, 2005, p. 81.

Serena loves fashion, and that shows in the daring, unique outfits she wears on the tennis court.

Venus and Serena have become two of the most successful siblings in the world of sports, and they have supported each other throughout their historic careers.

player. Even though the news media tried to portray their relationship in terms of a rivalry for family dominance, Serena never saw it that way. She has written that their bond as sisters was always more important to them than their tennis victories: "Venus and I are really blessed. Long before fans and reporters knew us, our parents taught us that our relationship is much more important than being successful in tennis or getting ahead in the world. Our friendship with each other and our other sisters is one of the most important and fun aspects of our lives."[40] The strength of Serena and Venus's relationship is something that has helped both sisters through difficult times on and off the tennis court.

Chapter Five

Personal Trials and Family Tragedy

Serena Williams began 2003 on a high note. Her victory in the Australian Open completed the Serena Slam, and the entire tennis world waited to see if she would extend her Grand Slam streak at the French Open in June. Martina Navratilova won six consecutive Grand Slam titles from 1983 through 1984, and Serena was two wins away from matching Navratilova's feat.

Serena ultimately did not match Navratilova's accomplishment.

Justine Henin-Hardenne is shown here shaking hands with Serena after defeating her at the 2003 French Open, ending her winnning streak at four Grand Slam titles.

Her streak ended with the Serena Slam, as she was defeated in the semifinals of the 2003 French Open by Justine Henin-Hardenne. The match was difficult for Serena because she was booed loudly and often by the crowd, and she admitted after the match that it was difficult to play under such hostile conditions.

Serena's struggles did not last long, however, as she successfully defended her Wimbledon title in July 2003. She faced Venus once again in the final, defeating her sister 4–6, 6–4, 6–2. The victory over her sister was even more bittersweet than usual for Serena because Venus played the match in pain from a pulled abdominal muscle. After the match, Isha Williams explained that both of her sisters suffered during the match: "They both had it pretty ... bad, but it might have been rougher on Serena. Playing someone you love who is in pain and still having to play your hardest because you want the [win] is a very, very difficult thing."[41]

That bittersweet victory was followed by more challenges for the sisters. Serena found herself dealing with a major injury not long after Venus was injured at Wimbledon. However, that injury proved to be far less devastating than a family tragedy that shook Serena to her core.

Freak Injury

After proving she was the best player in the world by winning five of six Grand Slam titles, Serena was at the peak of her fame in 2003. However, in late July, she suffered a freak injury that threatened everything she had worked so hard to gain. Although Serena did not state the actual cause of her injury for years, she revealed in her 2009 autobiography how she really injured herself:

I was out at a club in Los Angeles, dancing and partying and having a grand old time, but the foolish part was that I was doing it in heels … I went into this little spin move out there on the floor and I could feel something go in my knee. I did my move and thought, "Oh, no, Serena. This can't be good."[42]

Serena's dance move caused a partial tear in the quadriceps tendon in her left knee. She had surgery on August 1 to repair the tear, and doctors told her it would be two months before she could resume playing. One of the tournaments she would miss was the U.S. Open, in which she was the defending champion. Venus also sat out the Open because of her pulled abdominal muscle, which meant that someone other than Venus or Serena would win the tournament for the first time since 1998. Justine Henin-Hardenne, who had defeated Serena at the French Open, emerged victorious.

Tragic News

On September 14, Serena was in Toronto with her sister Lyndrea when they received terrible news: Their sister Yetunde Price had been murdered in Compton—not far from where Serena and Venus had played tennis while growing up.

The five Williams sisters had always been extremely close, even though Yetunde, Isha, and Lyndrea had a different father than Venus and Serena. Yetunde, who was 31 years old, trained as a nurse, and co-owned a hair salon, was shot to death while sitting in a car with a male companion in Compton. Serena deeply loved Yetunde. She claimed her older sister had been like a mother to her when they were growing up and became a close friend in later years. To make her sister's tragic death even worse, they had spent a lot of time together while Serena was recovering from her knee injury and had become closer than ever.

The four remaining Williams sisters flocked to California upon hearing the news—Serena and Lyn from Toronto, Isha from San Francisco, and Venus from the Florida home she shared with Serena. Their parents—Richard Williams and

Yetunde sometimes appeared with her younger sister at important events. She is shown here with Serena at the 2003 ESPY Awards.

Oracene Price—also flew there from the separate homes they had owned in Florida since divorcing in 2002. A family spokesperson issued a statement that praised Yetunde as a vital part of the family: "She was our nucleus and our rock ... and her death leaves a void that can never be filled."[43] Family members gathered not only to mourn their sister, but also to care for her three young sons—Jeffrey, Justus, and Jair.

Yetunde's death deeply affected Serena, who had more time than usual to think about the tragedy because she was unable to play tennis. In her autobiography, Serena explained how lost she was after her sister's death: "The next days and weeks were a blur, and I didn't want to bother my parents or sisters ... because it was such a private, painful time."[44]

Yetunde's death gave Serena a reason to extend her break from tennis. Although doctors had predicted she could be back in eight weeks, Serena did not return for eight months. Part of the reason for her long absence was that she was

"Too Impossible. Too Sad."

Serena Williams claims that one of the worst moments in her life was when she learned that her sister Yetunde Price had been shot to death in Los Angeles in September 2003. Serena was in Toronto, Canada, filming scenes for a television show when her sister was killed. She found out what happened when she called her sister's home. In her autobiography, Serena described the overwhelming sense of loss she felt when a cousin told her that her sister was dead:

> I thought, Gone? Tunde? It didn't make sense. I'd just spoken to her earlier in the day. [She had] just opened her own beauty salon and was finally starting to do well with it. She was only thirty-one years old, and I know it's a cliché but she really did have her whole life ahead of her. Gone? My sister? There was just no way. It was too crazy. Too impossible. Too sad. Her [three] children needed her. Her parents needed her. Her sisters needed her.[1]

1. Serena Williams with Daniel Paisner, *On the Line.* Boston, MA: Grand Central, 2009, p. 158.

grieving for her sister. Serena has also admitted that she did not mind stepping away from tennis for a longer period than her recovery was supposed to take because she had so many other interests to pursue.

Pursuing Other Interests

Although Venus and Serena never missed a Grand Slam event unless they were injured, they had always competed in fewer tournaments each year than most players. Some players and tennis officials criticized them for their limited schedules, claiming that the sisters were so popular that their absence was hurting the growth of their sport's fan base. Venus and Serena were able to play fewer tournaments because they made so much more money than most players. They were so talented that they earned a lot of money in the few tournaments they chose to play in, and they earned additional income from endorsements. For example, in 2004, Serena signed what was reported to be a five-year, $40 million contract with Nike to lend her name to a new line of tennis shoes and clothes.

That same year, Serena started her own designer clothing line; she named the company Aneres, which is her first name spelled backwards. In an interview, Serena showed the same brash confidence she displayed in playing tennis in describing her natural talent for designing clothes:

I'm an unbelievable designer. I don't know how I know and just do these things. I just start sketching and then I just know the colors and I always know the forecast. I know green and purple are going to be hot. I was born to be a designer. I worked hard to be a tennis player, I don't work hard to be a designer.[45]

Fashion, however, was just one of many interests Serena pursued outside of tennis. Serena once told a reporter, "I'm an

Fashion is one of the many interests Serena Williams has pursued off the tennis court.

actress, I'm a model and an athlete. I put athlete third on my list."[46] She and her sister Venus had both made television appearances for several years, and Serena began to pursue such opportunities more avidly than Venus. She acted on *The Wayne Brady Show* and lent her voice to the animated comedy series *The Simpsons*.

After her surgery, Serena admitted that she was happy that her recovery would allow her to do more than just play tennis. "I love tennis … and I really, really miss it," she told a reporter, "but in a way it is kind of a relief to see that, wow, this actually gives me a chance to do some other stuff, some acting especially."[47] Serena had wasted no time diving into such projects; she was in Toronto when her sister died to act in the Showtime series *Street Time*.

By not playing, Serena lost her top tennis ranking to Kim Clijsters in mid-2003 after having held the top spot for more than a year. As the months dragged on, people began to question if Serena would ever return to tennis and, if she did, whether she could still be good enough to be considered the best player in the sport.

Back on the Court

Serena has admitted her long absence from tennis was due in part to the fact that she had not emotionally recovered from Yetunde's death. "I went through the motions of grieving [for Yetunde], but I was still too numb and raw to really grieve. I cried, but the tears didn't really take me anywhere,"[48] she has written. Even though she was still struggling with her grief, she eventually forced herself to put aside her sorrow and begin training hard for a comeback.

Serena made a memorable return in late March 2004 in the Nasdaq-100 Open in Miami. She won the tournament by soundly beating Elena Dementieva 6–1, 6–1 in the title match. Even though Serena won that tournament and a second in Beijing, China, she had a dismal season by her own standards because she failed to win a Grand Slam event. Serena's most humbling defeat came in July, when low-ranked Maria Sharapova, who was only 17 years old, soundly defeated her 6–1, 6–4 in the title match to deny her a third straight Wimbledon championship.

Serena's U.S. Open experience two months later in September was perhaps more aggravating than Wimbledon because she blamed her 6–2, 4–6, 4–6 quarterfinal loss to Jennifer Capriati on sloppy officiating. In the opening game of the third set, an umpire ruled a ball she hit out of bounds even though television replays showed it was an inch inside the lines. The ruling denied her a point and upset her so much she went on to lose the match. In unusually strong language, Serena blasted the official, Mariana Alves: "I guess she went temporarily insane."[49]

Serena's victory at the 2005 Australian Open was a bright spot in a dark period in her career.

Even though the mistake was so glaring that tournament officials apologized to Serena the next day, she had still been eliminated from the tournament.

After Serena's struggles in 2004, some tennis observers and players were claiming she would never again be a force in women's tennis. One of the most cutting remarks about Serena's future was made by player Jelena Dokic, who claimed, "That story is over. I don't even hear comments about Serena anymore."[50]

At the 2005 Australian Open, though, Serena surprised

"No One Escapes the Humbling"

Sports Illustrated magazine has documented the life of Serena Williams from the time she emerged as a teenage tennis prodigy in the 1990s. Most articles have been glowing tributes to her talent and accomplishments. In 2004, however, journalist S.L. Price wrote that Serena's loss in the title match at Wimbledon to 17-year-old Maria Sharapova had stripped away the aura of invincibility that Serena had built up by dominating women's tennis for several years:

> No one escapes the humbling. That's clear now. Serena Williams had been tennis's great exception for so long [that many believed if] anyone could sidestep the sport's cruelest cycle, the wheel of succession that sends up a cold-eyed teen to stalk and harry the aging champion, it would be Serena ...
>
> [But] the 22-year-old Williams ... felt the wheel turn ... [when] Maria Sharapova, seeded 13th, beat Williams 6–1, 6–4 ...

everyone by regaining her old, dominating form to win the tournament. Even though she had to be treated for a rib injury during the first set, Serena beat Lindsay Davenport 2–6, 6–3, 6–0 to capture her sixth Grand Slam title.

That Grand Slam victory, however, did not lead to an immediate return to top form for Serena. She played so poorly the rest of the 2005 season that she dropped out of the top 10 rankings, and 2006 was even worse: She continued to falter due to injuries and her continuing inability to fully concentrate on tennis.

Over 73 minutes Sharapova stripped away Williams's armor, the hauteur [haughtiness] that has marked her in her prime, and the resulting sights and sounds were almost unimaginable: Williams slipping at the key moment of an epic rally and bouncing on her rear end; Williams, too startled to handle a laser-like Sharapova return, emitting a loud moan; Williams taking a ball on the nose after it ricocheted off her racket; Williams, down a break point at 4-4 in the second set, slipping again, on her way to the net, and whacking a forehand wide. Then there was Williams, never before at a loss for answers, meeting the press after the match and saying, "I just didn't ... I don't know what happened."[1]

Maria Sharapova was not famous when she beat Serena at Wimbledon in 2004, but she then became one of tennis's brightest young stars.

1. S.L. Price, "Splendor on the Grass," *Sports Illustrated*, July 12, 2004, www.si.com/vault/2004/07/12/376471/splendor-on-the-grass-in-two-memorable-wimbledon-finals-that-pumped-new-life-into-tennis-teenage-wonder-maria-sharapova-and-racket-wizard-roger-federer-conquered-americas-best.

Still Struggling

A major factor underlying Serena's decline was her continuing grief over the death of her sister, an emotion so strong that it drained her of her will to compete. In her autobiography, this is how she described it: "I was slipping into a depression. I don't think it was what a psychologist would have called a clinical depression, but it was an aching sadness, an all over weariness, a sudden disinterest in the world around me—in tennis, above all."[51]

Until Serena learned to work through her grief, she would be unable to regain her place as the best female tennis player in the world.

Chapter Six

Back on Top

In early 2005, Serena Williams addressed those who had begun to speculate that she and her sister would never again regain their status as the top players in tennis. Speaking to reporters during the Australian Open about the claims that she and Venus were on the decline in their careers, she said, "That's not fair—I'm tired of not saying anything ... We've been practicing hard. We've had serious injuries ... So no, we're not declining. We're here. I don't have to win this tournament to prove anything ... I know that I'm one of the best players out here."[52]

Serena backed up her statement with her victory in that Grand Slam event, but one victory did not make the speculation about her declining career stop. Instead, it only grew louder and more intense as she missed more tournaments and performed poorly in many of the ones she did participate in. By summer 2006, Serena was no longer one of the top 125 female players and was reaching the 140th spot in the rankings. As Karen Crouse of the *New York Times* put it, she had gone "from nearly invincible to almost invisible."[53]

Although some counted Serena out, she eventually turned her career around and reclaimed her spot at the top of her sport. How did she orchestrate such a strong comeback? She first began by turning her life around away from the tennis court.

Battling Depression

In January 2006, Serena failed to defend her Australian Open title when 17th-seeded Daniela Hantuchova beat her in straight sets in a third-round match. After returning to the United States, she did not play again until July. Although Serena claimed she was not playing because she was trying to get back in top form physically, the real reason she stayed away from tennis was because she was hurting emotionally. In her autobiography, Serena wrote, "I was depressed. Deeply and utterly and completely depressed. I didn't talk to anyone for weeks and weeks. I think I went a month and a half without talking to my mom, which was so out of character for me because we usually spoke every day. It freaked her out, I'm

Serena has taken many trips to Africa, and she has devoted much of her time away from tennis to helping Africans, especially young Africans, lead happy, safe, and healthy lives.

Choosing Tennis

In her autobiography, Serena openly discussed how she overcame depression. In this excerpt, she described how she was weighed down by the expectations placed on her by other people and how she began to climb out of the dark place she was in by choosing her own path:

Tennis was about the last thing on my mind. It didn't seem important ...

I didn't know it at the time, but I was slipping into a depression. I started seeing a therapist—weekly, at first, then a couple of times a week. The more I talked, the more I started to realize that my gloomy funk had to do with making other people happy. It came up because of Tunde [Yetunde]. It came up because of my knee injury. It came up because of all those weeks at number one, and the pressures I felt to get back there. It was all these things, but the main ingredient was me trying to please everyone else.

Then a weird and wonderful thing happened ... going back to when I was a kid, I'd never made an active or conscious choice where tennis was concerned. It was always like tennis chose me. Don't get me wrong, I was honored to have been chosen. But it had always been expected of me, and held out like a given. I came to it by default, and it took reaching for it here, when I was down and desperate, for me fully to embrace the game. I chose tennis. At last.[1]

1. Serena Williams, "Serena Williams: Queen of the Court: Extracts from Serena's Newly Published Autobiography," *The Guardian*, August 29, 2009. www.guardian.co.uk/sport/2009/aug/29/serena-williams-autobiography-extracts.

sure. I didn't talk to my sisters, and it freaked them out, too."[54]

Her despair was caused by a combination of her sister's death, the pressure she felt to be the world's best player, and the burden of trying to overcome a series of nagging injuries and return to tennis when she no longer cared about the sport as she once did. Eventually, she began going to therapy in Los Angeles, where she was living at the time. The therapy sessions helped her deal with her emotions in a healthy way and put things into perspective.

Serena was also affected in a positive way by a humanitarian trip she took to Africa in November 2006. On that trip, Serena met with women and children living in Senegal, as well as the president of the country. Serena has said that seeing an island off Senegal from which Africans were shipped to the United States as slaves reminded her that, as a descendant of slaves, she could survive any hardship. "That just changed me," Serena has said. "It gave me strength and courage, and it let me know that I can endure anything."[55]

Serena has written that as her mood improved, she gradually began to be excited about tennis again. In January 2007, Serena took her new determination to succeed in the sport to the Australia Open. Once again, that tournament played a pivotal part in her career.

From the Bottom Back to the Top

Serena arrived in Australia ranked 81st in the world, but she defeated Maria Sharapova 6–1, 6–2 in the Open to win her eighth Grand Slam title. After she won, she told the cheering fans, "I would like to dedicate this win to my sister, who is not here. Her name is Yetunde. I just love her so much."[56]

The win surprised the tennis world, which had believed Serena was past her prime. Then, in May, Serena proved that her new determination to succeed was no fluke when she won the Sony Ericsson Open in Miami by beating the world's top-ranked player, Justine Henin-Hardenne, in the title match. The 25-year-old was now boldly proclaiming that she was again the best player in the world.

However, it would take her two more years of hard work and dedication to reclaim the top ranking in tennis. Hampered by knee and thumb injuries, Serena failed to win another tournament in 2007. The next year, though, a healthy Serena defeated Jelena Jankovic to win the U.S. Open for her ninth Grand Slam title. The victory helped her recapture the top spot in the rankings. Serena also won a gold medal with Venus in women's doubles at the Beijing Olympics, which was their second doubles gold medal. Their first came in 2000 at the Olympic Games in Sydney, Australia.

Despite Serena's successful year, Jankovic reclaimed the top ranking in October, and 2008 ended with Jankovic ranked first and Serena second. That made Serena more determined than ever to be the best, and in 2009, she won the Australian Open and Wimbledon to reclaim the title of the world's best female tennis player. Although she once again regained the top ranking she had chased for so long, she lost it after only a few weeks to Dinara Safina. That happened because Serena chose not to

By 2010, Serena had once again reached the top of the tennis world.

play in certain tournaments, and Safina won enough points to surpass her. However, Serena still won $6,545,586 to set a new single-season earnings record for a female tennis player. Her big year pushed her career earnings to more than $23 million, a record for a female athlete in any sport. The Associated Press news agency named her the Female Athlete of the Year in 2009. In a story on the honor, Stacey Allaster of the Women's Tennis Association complimented Serena by saying, "We can attribute the strength and the growth of women's tennis a great deal to her. She is a superstar."[57]

In January 2010, Serena again won the Australian Open, and she went into Wimbledon as the world's top female tennis player once again. On July 3, 2010, Serena proved she was the world's best player by winning Wimbledon for the second straight year. After easily defeating Vera Zvonareva in the final 6–3, 6–2, Serena lifted both arms in the air in victory. She then held up all 10 fingers, closed her hands, and then raised and wiggled 3 fingers in the air. The gesture stood for the number 13, the number of Grand Slam titles she had won in her career to that point.

Health Scares

Serena's quest for more Grand Slam titles in 2010 was cut short once again by injury. On July 7, 2010, just days after her Wimbledon victory, she cut her feet while stepping on glass as she left a restaurant in Germany, and she eventually needed surgery to repair a tendon that had been sliced. She missed the 2010 U.S. Open and also the 2011 Australian Open because of this injury.

While rehabbing from these injuries, Serena suffered an even more serious health problem. In February 2011, Serena was hospitalized for a pulmonary embolism, also known as blood clots in her lungs. She had to have surgery to remove the clots, and she had to receive injections of blood-thinning medication to make sure the clots did not come back.

One of the injections affected a blood vessel in Serena's abdomen, causing blood to build up under the skin and form a lump.

Serena Loses Her Cool

Serena Williams's fantastic 2009 season was marred by an angry outburst she had in September at the U.S. Open. During her semifinal loss to Kim Clijsters, Serena exploded in anger when a line judge ruled she had made a foot fault, meaning her foot was over the baseline. The decision cost Williams a point, and she shouted obscenities at the line judge. Tennis officials fined her a record $82,500 for her rant and put her on probation, warning her that another outburst could cost her more money and potentially a chance to play in the next U.S. Open.

The profanity seemed out of character for Serena, and *Sports Illustrated* writer S.L. Price wrote that the incident was so ugly that it could forever affect the way fans and tennis historians view her:

> *What I saw was her raising her racket in what looked like a menacing posture, though she may not have understood this at the time. But after having heard what she did say, she clearly was verbally threatening the lineswoman, and combined with the fact that she had a ball in one hand and was raising her racket over her head with the other, I don't blame the lineswoman for feeling a bit fearful. [She is certainly] a great player, but this is going to be a great blight on her career. No question about it.*[1]

1. S.L. Price, "How Does Her U.S. Open Implosion Change Serena's Legacy?" *Sports Illustrated*, September 13, 2009. www.si.com/more-sports/2009/09/13/serena-qa.

The lump—also called a hematoma—was surgically removed, and she then had to spend a lot of time recovering at home under the supervision of a team of doctors.

Turning 30 years old in 2011, Serena was not old for an average person, but not many tennis players improve after 30. From July 2010 to June 2011, Serena spent 11 months off the court because of injuries and illness. During this time, she found a new appreciation for tennis, and she missed playing the sport: "I am so excited to be healthy enough to compete again," she said in a statement announcing her return to tennis. "These past 12 months have been extremely tough and character building. I have so much to be grateful for. I'm thankful to my family, friends, and fans for all of their support. Serena's back!"[58]

As excited as Serena was to get back onto the court, coming back from tough injuries and serious illness would not be easy. In July 2011, her ranking dropped to 175. Tennis fans around the world wondered if Serena's career was going to head downhill or if could she come back once again.

Serena started slowly. In her first tournament back, at Eastbourne, England, she lost in the second round. Then, at Wimbledon, she made it to the fourth round, but she lost to Marion Bartoli of France. She avenged the loss by beating Bartoli in the final at the Bank of the West Classic in Stanford, California.

Serena returned to tennis in 2011 after nearly a year away from the sport she loved.

Blood Clots

Flying around the country—or the world—on long-distance flights might sound glamorous, but sitting in a plane for hours at a time reduces a person's blood flow. In addition to Serena, many other professional athletes have had pulmonary embolisms (blood clots) or related health problems. These athletes include basketball player Chris Bosh, hockey player Steven Stamkos, and speed skater Rebekah Bradford. Athletes also have a much lower resting blood pressure and heart rate than normal people. This is an advantage during competition, because although their blood pressure rises, it is still in a healthier zone than it would be for average people exerting a comparable amount of energy. However, it also means that while resting, athletes' blood flows more slowly and can clog up their veins, especially if they sit for long periods of time.

If left untreated, blood clots result in death as much as 30 percent of the time. Former professional basketball player Jerome Kersey died from a blood clot in 2015. That is why it is important to get up and walk around when sitting for long periods of time, such as during long flights. Stretching also gets blood flowing in your muscles and can prevent blood clots.

It was Serena's first tournament win since the 2010 French Open, which was more than a year earlier.

At the U.S. Open, Serena made the final, this time against Samantha Stosur of Australia. She had beaten Stosur to win the Rogers Cup in Canada a month earlier. This time, however, Stosur won. However, simply making the U.S. Open final was a great achievement for Serena after the health scares she had suffered.

Serena still was not at the top of her game, though. At the 2012 Australian Open, she made it to the fourth round, but things would go downhill later in 2012.

Finding a New Coach

The 2012 French Open was Serena's worst performance at a Grand Slam tournament at that point in her career. Arriving at the tournament as the fifth seed, Serena lost in the first round to Virginie Razzano, who was ranked 111th. It was the first time Serena had lost in the first round of a Grand Slam tournament. She had not even lost in the first round when she was a teenager. After this devastating result, something had to change, and Serena needed to revitalize her career, which was not an easy thing to do for anyone, much less a 30-year-old.

After her French Open loss, Serena hired a new coach, Patrick Mouratoglou. She asked him if she could train at his academy outside Paris. His plan was for Serena to get her focus back on the court, to forget about her injuries, and to get the most out of her ability. He thought her game was unbeatable, but sometimes she could get too nervous and uptight. Her biggest opponent was herself.

The results were immediate. In July 2012, Serena won her

Serena and Patrick Mouratoglou have developed a successful working relationship since she first hired him in 2012.

Speaking French

During her career, Serena worked hard to learn French, but she was too shy to try speaking French in public and with the media. Training with Mouratoglou, who is from France and speaks French, ultimately helped Serena feel more comfortable speaking the language publicly. At the awards ceremonies after the finals of the French Open in 2013, 2015, and 2016, Serena gave speeches to the crowd completely in French after accepting her trophies, even when she lost the final in 2016. Crowds at the Australian Open, Wimbledon, and U.S. Open speak English, but French Open crowds are appreciative when tennis players give speeches in French instead of English. Serena also speaks some Italian and has used it to address Italian crowds.

fifth Wimbledon title. She followed that up by winning two gold medals at the 2012 London Olympics, beating Sharapova in the singles final and winning the doubles final with Venus. Then, at the 2012 U.S. Open, Serena had one of her most dominant performances ever. She only lost one set on the way to winning her fourth U.S. Open.

Staying on Top

Serena entered 2013 on a 12-match winning streak. Her game was as good as it had been earlier in her career, when she was regularly winning Grand Slam tournaments. After winning a warm-up tournament in Brisbane, Australia, she lost in the quarterfinals of the 2013 Australian Open. However, she had earned enough points to secure the top spot in the women's tennis rankings, and she was just getting started. Over the 2013 season, she won 11 tournaments, more than any player had won in a single season since Martina Hingis won 12 in 1997. It was the best season of Serena's career to that point. Serena was becoming more dominant in her 30s than she had been in her 20s.

Serena was especially dominant on clay. She was undefeated on the surface, winning all five clay court tournaments she played in, tallying a 28–0 record. This included another French Open victory over Maria Sharapova.

After losing in the fourth round of Wimbledon, Serena played Victoria Azarenka in the final of the U.S. Open. The two split the first pair of sets, both closely played, but Serena overwhelmed Azarenka in the final set to win 7–5, 6–7, 6–1, defending her title and winning her fifth U.S. Open.

Serena won more than 95 percent of her matches in 2013, winning 78 and only losing 4. This was one of the greatest seasons any tennis player has ever had.

Another Serena Slam

After Serena's incredible 2013 season, it was tough to match that success in 2014, but Serena still won seven tournaments. She maintained the top ranking for the whole year, which was something no woman had done since the great Steffi Graf had done it in 1996. Serena ended the Grand Slam season in 2014 with a U.S. Open victory, setting the stage for what would prove to be another exciting run to a Serena Slam.

Serena picked up 2015 right where she left off 2014, winning the Australian Open 6–3, 7–6 over Maria Sharapova. It was Serena's sixth Australian Open win and her 19th Grand Slam singles title overall, which placed her second in Grand Slam singles titles in the Open era (after 1968), behind only Steffi Graf, who had 22 titles. Serena was now bearing down on records held by the all-time greats.

Serena then went back to Indian Wells for the first time since 2001, when she was showered with boos from the crowd after Venus pulled out of their semifinal match with an injury. Serena used her Indian Wells return to bring light to the issue of legal representation for people who cannot afford quality legal counsel. Her return kicked off fundraising for the Equal Justice Initiative, which works to fund legal representation for poor defendants and prisoners. She raised money for the initiative by raffling off a chance to sit in her VIP box during the tournament. Unfortunately, a cruel coincidence awaited Serena at Indian Wells. After playing at a high level throughout the tournament, Serena injured her knee and had to withdraw before her semifinal match.

After Indian Wells, Serena rested during most of the clay court season, but she came back with a bang, winning the French Open. This was a grueling tournament, as Serena went to three sets in most of her matches, but she battled back time and time again, ultimately winning the title over Lucie Safarova 6–3, 6–7, 6–2 in the final.

Serena arrived at Wimbledon with a chance to duplicate her 2002 achievement, the Serena Slam, winning four Grand Slam titles in a row over two years. Serena did not disappoint, dominating the tournament, only losing two sets and winning the title 6–4, 6–4 over Garbiñe Muguruza of Spain, an opponent more than a decade younger than Serena.

The sports world greatly anticipated the 2015 U.S. Open.

Serena had a very successful 2015.

Since Serena had won the first three Grand Slam tournaments that year, she had a chance to win all four in one year and be the first player to complete the calendar-year Grand Slam since Steffi Graf did so in 1988. Even Serena was thinking about topping her own Serena Slam with a calendar-year Grand Slam. After winning Wimbledon, she speculated about what it would mean to achieve the feat on what was essentially her home court: "It would be really good to have this opportunity to go into New York being American with that amazing New York crowd," she said. "Hopefully, people would be really cheering me on, to like push me over the edge and give me that extra strength I need to go for this historic moment."[59]

Serena started the U.S. Open tournament very well, only losing one set in her first four matches, but in her quarterfinal win against Venus, she lost another set, winning 6–2, 1–6, 6–3. Then, after a strong start and a first-set win in her semifinal match against veteran player Roberta Vinci, she began to struggle. Vinci won the last two sets and the match, 2–6, 6–4, 6–4, ending Serena's calendar Grand Slam hopes.

Serena was disappointed, but she was complimentary to Vinci, another veteran player and a contemporary of Serena's at age 33. "She's going for it at a late stage," Serena said. "So that's good for her to keep going for it and playing so well. Actually, I guess it's inspiring. But, yeah, I think she played literally out of her mind."[60]

Despite failing to accomplish a calendar-year Grand Slam, Serena still ended 2015 as the top-ranked female tennis player in the world, and she had completed another Serena Slam at an age when most other tennis players would be declining in their performance. Because of her incredible year, *Sports Illustrated* magazine named Serena its Sportsperson of the Year for 2015. In explaining the magazine's reasons behind the choice, S.L. Price described why 2015 was such a monumental year for the tennis star:

All year Williams kept coming, on a path more arduous than anyone knew, and she put together the best season by a woman in a quarter century. "I do want to be known as the greatest ever," she says. To many she already is. But that's not the sole reason why we arrive, now, at this honor. It's also because Williams kept pushing herself to grow, to be better, and tennis was the least of it. The trying is what's impressive. The trying is why we are here.[61]

2016 and Beyond

In 2016, Serena kept her high level of play going. At the Australian Open, Serena made yet another Grand Slam final. However, Serena met her match in that final, as Angelique Kerber of Germany used a defensive game to frustrate Williams and win 6–4, 3–6, 6–4.

At the French Open, Serena again reached the final in dominant fashion. However, she was also defeated again in a Grand Slam final, this time by the play of Garbiñe Muguruza, who she had defeated at Wimbledon one year earlier. For Muguruza, who was only 22 years old, this was an immense milestone, as she has stated that Serena was one of her tennis idols growing up.

At Wimbledon, everything finally came together for Serena. She cruised to her seventh Wimbledon title, only losing one set. In the final, she avenged her loss at the Australian Open by defeating Kerber 7–5, 6–3. Serena played much more aggressively than she did in Australia, and it paid off. With the win, she tied Steffi Graf for most Open-era Grand Slam titles, with 22.

After the win, Serena talked about how much the chase for 22 titles had been on her mind. "Yeah, it's been incredibly difficult not to think about it," she said. "I had a couple of tries this year. But it makes the victory even sweeter to know how hard I worked for it."[62]

Serena then competed at the 2016 Olympics in Rio de Janeiro, Brazil, but she was unable to defend her Olympic titles there. Surprisingly, Venus and Serena lost in the first round of the doubles tournament, and Serena lost in the third round of

Serena Williams's excellent play continued in 2016, showing the world that she has no plans to give up the sport she has dominated for more than a decade.

singles play. She then took time off to rest her shoulder after the Olympics.

Injuries also plagued Serena at the 2016 U.S. Open. Her left knee was injured in the tournament, and it was a factor in her semifinal loss to Karolina Pliskova. Pliskova's victory denied Serena the chance to break Graff's record of most Grand Slam titles in the Open era, a feat which she was left to chase again with the start of the 2017 season.

For many tennis fans, the question at the back of their minds is one Serena keeps challenging with each victory: How long will she continue to play, delighting crowds with her powerful presence and dominating skill? When asked about retirement

Serena at the Olympics

Representing her country at the Olympics has always been important to Serena. She has competed in four Olympic Games: the 2000 Olympics in Sydney, the 2008 Olympics in Beijing, the 2012 Olympics in London, and the 2016 Olympics in Rio. In 2000, 2008, and 2012, she won gold medals with Venus in doubles, and she won singles gold in 2012. (She missed the 2004 Olympics in Athens with a knee injury.)

Serena is passionate about the Olympic experience. "[My collection of Olympic medals] is probably one thing I have that I love the most," she told *USA Today* before the 2016 Olympics. "My experience has been really amazing at the Olympics. I really loved going out there and competing, really just, you know, standing out there and being an Olympic athlete."[1]

1. Quoted in Nick McCarvel, "Serena Williams Says It's 'Sad' Athletes Will Skip Rio," *USA Today*, June 28, 2016. www.usatoday.com/story/sports/olympics/rio-2016/2016/06/28/serena-williams-rio-olympics-zika-virus/86467034/.

during the 2016 U.S. Open, Serena did not sound like she was going to give up tennis any time soon: "I'm still having fun out there. I'm still able to compete with the best. I think that's what matters most for me. I just am not ready to throw in the towel yet or just to have enough yet."[63]

With that attitude, it seems Serena Williams has no plans to slow down any time soon.

Beyond the World of Sports

Tennis is not the only thing that keeps Serena in the spotlight. She has many endorsement deals, business ventures, and other interests that have helped her become not just a famous athlete, but a worldwide celebrity.

Serena has been featured in advertisements for Nike and Gatorade, among other products. She also sells a line of clothing, jewelry, and purses on the Home Shopping Network. Another business venture Serena is involved with is the Miami Dolphins of the National Football League (NFL). Both she and Venus became minority owners of the team in 2009, which made them the first African American women to purchase any stake in an NFL team. In 2016, it was announced that she and her sister also invested in the Ultimate Fighting Championship (UFC), a mixed marital arts promotion company.

One of Serena's favorite non-tennis activities is acting. Serena has made guest appearances on many television talk shows, dramas, and comedies. She and Venus even had their own real-ity show called *Venus and Serena: For Real*, which aired for one season in 2005. Serena also famously appeared in the music video for Beyoncé's song "Sorry," which was part of the singer's visual album *Lemonade*.

Serena has also become deeply involved with various

Serena and Venus are shown here at a 2004 charity event with another pair of famous sisters: Haylie and Hilary Duff.

"To All Incredible Women Who Strive for Excellence"

In November 2016, Serena wrote an open letter that was published in *Porter* magazine. In the letter, Serena spoke about gender equality and equal pay, which is an issue that is very important to her:

To all incredible women who strive for excellence,

... When I was growing up, I had a dream. I'm sure you did, too. My dream wasn't like that of an average kid, my dream was to be the best tennis player in the world. Not the best "female" tennis player in the world ...

But as we know, too often women are not supported enough or are discouraged from choosing their path. I hope together we can change that ...

So when the subject of equal pay comes up, it frustrates me because I know firsthand that I, like you, have done the same work and made the same sacrifices as our male counterparts. I would never want

charitable causes and humanitarian organizations, using her place in the spotlight and the money she has earned to help those who need it. The Serena Williams Fund raises money that is used to help at-risk young people get scholarships, to build schools in Africa (including the Serena Williams Secondary School in Kenya), and to support the work UNICEF does for children around the world. Serena was named a UNICEF Goodwill Ambassador in 2011. She has also become an advocate against gun violence and has donated money to help families who have been affected by gun violence.

my daughter to be paid less than my son for the same work. Nor would you.

As we know, women have to break down many barriers on the road to success. One of those barriers is the way we are constantly reminded we are not men, as if it is a flaw. People call me one of the "world's greatest female athletes". Do they say LeBron [James] is one of the world's best male athletes? Is Tiger [Woods]? [Roger] Federer? Why not? They are certainly not female. We should never let this go unchallenged. We should always be judged by our achievements, not by our gender.

For everything I've achieved in my life, I am profoundly grateful to have experienced the highs and lows that come with success. It is my hope that my story, and yours, will inspire all young women out there to push for greatness and follow their dreams with steadfast resilience. We must continue to dream big, and in doing so, we empower the next generation of women to be just as bold in their pursuits.[1]

1. Serena Williams, "'We Must Continue to Dream Big': An Open Letter From Serena Williams," *The Guardian*, November 29, 2016. www.theguardian.com/lifeandstyle/2016/nov/29/dream-big-open-letter-serena-williams-porter-magazine-incredible-women-of-2016-issue-women-athletes.

Serena continues to use her platform to speak out about social issues, such as racism, sexism, and body shaming. Although some may prefer for her to only talk about her sport, many see her as a role model for daring to speak out about problems facing many people, especially women and people of color. As Andrew Eichenholz of *Rolling Stone* magazine wrote,

Sure, Serena has not been the only athlete to comment on social issues. But there is far more to Williams' world than tennis—win or lose. A 22nd Grand Slam title was important and her on-court career will inspire countless children and fans in general to play

the sport, but she has consistently painted the line with winners by proving another point—it is not all about tennis. For that, she will always be a champion.[64]

Making an Impact

Serena Williams does not shy away from talking about her legacy, and, in doing so, she has started an honest conversation about how we talk about female athletes. For example, when a reporter asked Serena how she feels about being considered "one of the greatest female athletes of all time," she responded, "I prefer the words 'one of the greatest athletes of all time.'"[65]

Serena Williams seems poised to continue to build her legacy long after her tennis career is over.

Serena Williams should be known to history not as a great female athlete, but as a great athlete. Her long and dominant career is one that any athlete—male or female—would be proud to have. From her time on the courts of Compton to her successes on tennis's biggest stages, Serena has proven that it does not matter where a person comes from or what they look like—even in a sport as traditionally wealthy and white as tennis. What matters are talent and determination. Serena certainly has shown both over the course of her career. The legacy of her and her sister Venus is one of breaking barriers and inspiring a new demographic of young people to enjoy a sport that once seemed off-limits to them.

Serena is a game-changer. Her confidence, her skills, and even her clothes have made an impact on the sport she grew up playing. Her desire to speak out about social issues and work to help others has made her a role model even for those who have never held a tennis racket. Because of this, she is more than just a great female athlete who has left her mark on her sport; she is a great athlete who has left her mark on the world beyond the tennis courts where she first earned her fame.

Notes

Introduction: A Superstar On and Off the Court

1. Billie Jean King, "Serena Williams," *TIME*, April 29, 2010. content.time.com/time/specials/packages/article/0,28804,1984685_1984949_1985247,00.html.

2. Claudia Rankne, "The Meaning of Serena Williams," *New York Times*, August 25, 2015. www.nytimes.com/2015/08/30/magazine/the-meaning-of-serena-williams.html.

3. Quoted in Peter Hossli, "I'm a Thinker," Hossli.com, January 4, 2008. www.hossli.com/articles/2008/01/04/serena-williams-im-a-thinker/.

Chapter One: All in the Tennis Family

4. Serena Williams with Daniel Paisner, *On the Line*. New York, NY: Grand Central Publishing, 2009, dedication page.

5. Williams with Paisner, *On the Line*, p. 77.

6. Williams with Paisner, *On the Line*, p. 77.

7. Venus and Serena Williams with Hilary Beard, *Venus & Serena: Serving from the Hip, 10 Rules for Living, Loving and Winning*. Boston, MA: Houghton Mifflin, 2005, p. 3.

8. Quoted in Sonja Steptoe, "Child's Play," *Sports Illustrated*, June 10, 1991. www.si.com/vault/1991/06/10/124343/childs-play-tenniss-newest-pixie-is-named-venus-at-age-10-she-dreams-of-flying-to-jupiter-others-have-earthier-hopes-for-her.

9. Serena Williams, "Serena Williams: Queen of the Court: Extracts from Serena's Newly Published Autobiography," *The Guardian*. August 29, 2009. www.guardian.co.uk/sport/2009/aug/29/serena-williams-autobiography-extracts.

10. Quoted in Williams with Paisner, *On the Line*, p. 51.

11. Quoted in S.L. Price, "Who's Your Daddy?," *Sports Illustrated*, May 31, 1999. www.si.com/vault/1999/05/31/8107824/whos-your-daddy-call-richard-williams-what-you-wantbizarre-deceitful-or-perhaps-madbut-be-sure-of-one-thing-he-has-brilliantly-guided-the-careers-and-lives-of-his-daughters-venus-and-serena-the-hottest-players-in-tennis.

Chapter Two: Training for the Pros

12. Quoted in Steptoe, "Child's Play."

13. Quoted in Williams with Paisner, *On the Line*, p. 95.

14. Williams with Paisner, *On the Line*, p. 103.

15. Williams with Paisner, *On the Line*, p. 101.

16. Quoted in Price, "Who's Your Daddy?"

17. Quoted in Dave Rineberg, *Venus & Serena: My Seven Years as Hitting Coach for the Williams Sisters.* Hollywood, FL: Frederick Fell, 2001, p. 29.

18. Quoted in Robert McG. Thomas Jr., "Double-Barreled Debuts; Williams Sisters Join the Family Circle," *New York Times*, April 6, 1992. www.nytimes.com/1992/04/06/sports/side-lines-double-barreled-debuts-williams-sisters-join-the-family-circle.html.

19. Quoted in Robin Finn, "Never Too Young for Tennis Millions," *New York Times*, November 10, 1993. www.nytimes.com/1993/11/10/sports/tennis-never-too-young-for-tennis-millions.html.

20. Quoted in Rineberg, *Venus & Serena*, p. 40.

Chapter Three: From the Sidelines to the Court

21. Williams with Paisner, *On the Line*, p. 114.

22. Quoted in Robin Finn, "Tennis: A Family Tradition at Age 14," *New York Times*, October 31, 1995. www.nytimes.com/1995/10/31/sports/tennis-a-family-tradition-at-age-14.html.

23. Quoted in Rineberg, *Venus & Serena*, p. 105.

24. Quoted in Finn, "Tennis: A Family Tradition at Age 14."

25. Quoted in S.L. Price, "Venus Envy," *Sports Illustrated*, September 15, 1997. www.si.com/vault/1997/09/15/231783/venus-envy-martina-hingis-and-patrick-rafter-reigned-at-the-us-open-but-the-play-of-venus-williams-was-the-bigger-story-much-to-her-peers-dismay.

26. Quoted in Joy Duckett Cain and Tamala Edwards, "At the Top of Their Game," *Essence*, August 1998, p. 78.

27. Quoted in "Consolation for Williamses," *New York Times*, June 7, 1999. www.nytimes.com/1999/06/07/sports/tennis-a-consolation-for-williamses.html.

28. Quoted in Robin Finn, "Williams Showdown: Venus Beats Sister Serena," *New York Times*, March 29, 1999. www.nytimes.com/1999/03/29/sports/tennis-williams-showdown-venus-beats-sister-serena.html.

29. Quoted in "Covering Serena Williams Through the Years," *New York Times*, August 30, 2015. www.nytimes.com/2015/08/31/sports/covering-serena-williams-through-the-years.html?_r=0.

30. Quoted in Robin Finn, "U.S. Open; Unstoppable Team Willams Takes Doubles Title," *New York Times*, September 13, 1999. www.nytimes.com/1999/09/13/sports/us-open-unstoppable-team-williams-takes-doubles-title.html.

Chapter Four: Four in a Row: The Serena Slam

31. Quoted in Peter Bodo, "Revisiting Serena's Slam Titles: Serena

Beats Venus in Chase for Glory," ESPN.com, August 26, 2015. www.espn.com/tennis/usopen15/story/_/id/13484210/tennis-revisiting-serena-williams-grand-slam-titles-nos-1-5.

32. Quoted in Selena Roberts, "Venus Williams Wins Sisters' Showdown," *New York Times*, July 7, 2000. www.nytimes.com/2000/07/07/sports/tennis-venus-williams-wins-sisters-showdown.html.

33. Quoted in Selena Roberts, "Serena Williams Shows She Can Be Composed, Too," *New York Times*, June 9, 2002. www.nytimes.com/2002/06/09/sports/tennis-serena-williams-shows-she-can-be-composed-too.html.

34. L. Jon Wertheim, "Serves & Follies," *Sports Illustrated*, July 15, 2002. www.si.com/vault/2015/07/16/8106420/serves--follies-at-the-weirdest-wimbledon-in-ages-form-finally-held-as-topranked-lleyton-hewitt-and-serena-williams-cut-down-the-opposition.

35. Quoted in Selena Roberts, "Serena Williams Shows Confidence and Flair," *New York Times*, September 9, 2009. www.nytimes.com/2002/09/09/sports/tennis-serena-williamsshows-confidence-and-flair.html.

36. Quoted in Christopher Clarey, "A Slam to Call Her Own," *New York Times*, January 25, 2003. www.nytimes.com/2003/01/25/sports/tennis-a-slam-to-call-her-own.html.

37. Quoted in Selena Roberts, "Serena Williams Wins as the Boos Pour Down," *New York Times*, March 18, 2001. www.nytimes.com/2001/03/18/sports/tennis-serena-williams-wins-as-the-boos-pour-down.html.

38. Quoted in Roberts, "Serena Williams Wins as the Boos Pour Down."

39. Quoted in Selena Roberts, "The Williams Sisters Let 'er Rip," *New York Times*, July 7, 2002. www.nytimes.com/2002/07/07/sports/tennis-the-williams-sisters-let-er-rip.html.

40. Venus and Serena Williams with Hilary Beard, *Serving from the Hip,* p. 3.

Chapter Five: Personal Trials and Family Tragedy

41. Quoted in S.L. Price, "Nerves and Volleys," *Sports Illustrated*, July 14, 2003. www.si.com/vault/2003/07/14/346176/nerves-and-volleys-serena-williams-won-another-ragged-final-against-sister-venus-to-defend-her-wimbledon-title-and-roger-federer-bagged-his-first-major-with-flawless-all-court-tennis.

42. Williams with Paisner, *On the Line*, p. 164.

43. Quoted in Richard Faussett, Lisa Dillman, and Scott Glover, "Tennis Star's Sister Killed in Shooting," *Los Angeles Times*, September 15, 2003. articles.latimes.com/2003/sep/15/local/me-williams15.

44. Williams with Paisner, *On the Line*, p. 161.

45. Quoted in Associated Press, "Serena Williams Keen on Fashion Career," Fox News, November 14, 2004. www.foxnews.com/story/0,2933,138502,00.html.

46. Quoted in Mary Ormsby, "Death Has Sisters Pondering Future," *Toronto Star*, September 21, 2003, p. E5.

47. Quoted in Christopher Clarey, "Williamses Test a Life Without Any Games," *New York Times*, August 28, 2003. www.nytimes.com/2003/08/28/sports/tennis-williamses-test-a-life-withoutany-games.html/.

48. Williams with Paisner, *On the Line*, p. 166.

49. Quoted in Francie Grace, "Controversy Mars Key Open Match," CBS News, September 7, 2004. www.cbsnews.com/news/controversy-mars-key-open-match/.

50. Quoted in Tom Fordyce, "Serena's Biggest Test," BBC Sports, March 24, 2004. news.bbc.co.uk/sport2/hi/tennis/3563759.stm.

51. Williams with Paisner, *On the Line*, p. 173.

Chapter Six: Back on Top

52. Quoted in "Angry Williams Rejects Criticism," BBC Sports, January 25, 2005. news.bbc.co.uk/sport2/hi/tennis/4204449.stm.

53. Karen Crouse, "Serena Williams Wins U.S. Open, Retaking No. 1," *New York Times*, September 7, 2008. www.nytimes.com/2008/09/08/sports/tennis/08women.html.

54. Williams with Paisner, *On the Line*, p. 175.

55. Quoted in Alex Tresniowski, "Serena, Serene," *People*, March 19, 2007. people.com/archive/serena-serene-vol-67-no-11/.

56. Quoted in Christopher Clarey, "Williams Shocks Sharapova to Win Australian Open," *New York Times*, January 27, 2007. www.nytimes.com/2007/01/27/sports/27iht-web.0127tennis.4368100.html.

57. Quoted in Associated Press, "Tennis No. 1 Serena is Top Female Athlete," ESPN.com, December 22, 2009. www.espn.com/sports/tennis/news/story?id=4764170.

58. Quoted in Christopher Clarey, "Serena Williams Returning to Tour," *New York Times*, June 6, 2011. www.nytimes.com/2011/06/07/sports/tennis/serena-williams-plans-to-play-at-wimbledon.html.

59. Quoted in Christopher Clarey, "Wimbledon 2015: Serena Williams Defeats Garbiñe Muguruza and Closes In on Grand Slam," *New York Times*, July 11, 2015. www.nytimes.com/2015/07/12/sports/tennis/wimbledon-2015-serena-williams-defeats-garbine-muguruza-and-closes-in-on-grand-slam.html.

60. Quoted in Christopher Clarey, "Roberta Vinci Ends Serena Williams's Grand Slam Bid at U.S. Open," *New York Times*, September 11, 2015. www.nytimes.com/2015/09/12/sports/tennis/roberta-vinci-ends-serena-williamss-grand-slam-run-at-us-open.html.

61. S.L. Price, "Serena Williams Is Sports Illustrated's

2015 Sportsperson of the Year," *Sports Illustrated*, December 14, 2015. www.si.com/sportsperson/2015/12/14/serena-williams-si-sportsperson-year.

62. Quoted in ESPN.com news service, "Serena Williams Wins Wimbledon to Tie Open Era Record with 22nd Slam Title," ESPN.com, July 9, 2016. www.espn.com/tennis/wimbledon16/story/_/id/16922072/2016-wimbledon-serena-williams-wins-22nd-grand-slam-title-tie-steffi-graf-open-era-record.

63. Quoted in Gatto Luigi, "Serena Williams, 'I'm Not Ready to Throw in the Towel, I Am Still Having Fun Out There,'" *Tennis World*, May 9, 2016. www.tennisworldusa.org/news/news/Serena_Williams/35966/serena-williams-i-m-not-ready-to-throw-in-the-towel-i-am-still-having-fun-out-there-/.

64. Andrew Eichenholz, "How Serena Williams Is Using Her Star Power for Good," *Rolling Stone*, July 11, 2016. www.rollingstone.com/sports/news/serena-williams-using-her-star-power-for-social-good-20160711.

65. Quoted in Dayna Evans, "Serena Williams Prefers to Be Known As One of the Greatest Athletes of All Time," The Cut (*New York*), July 7, 2016. nymag.com/thecut/2016/07/serena-williams-best-female-athlete.html.

Serena Williams Year by Year

1981
On September 26, Serena Jameka Williams is born in Saginaw, Michigan.

1991
Richard Williams pulls Venus and Serena Williams from junior competition and in September, moves his family to Florida so his daughters can enroll in the Rick Macci Tennis Academy.

1992
Venus and Serena play against each other in an exhibition doubles match at the Family Circle Magazine Cup in Hilton Head, South Carolina. Their partners are pro tennis stars Billie Jean King and Rosie Casals.

1995
Serena loses to Annie Miller in her professional debut at the Bell Challenge in Quebec City, Canada.

1999
Serena wins her first tournament, the Gaz de France in Paris; graduates from high school; wins the French Open doubles title with Venus; and wins her first Grand Slam singles title at the U.S. Open.

2002
Serena defeats Venus in the finals of three Grand Slam events: the French Open, Wimbledon, and the U.S. Open.

2003
On January 25, in the Australian Open finals, Serena again beats Venus to complete the Serena Slam; Serena has surgery on her knee and does not return to tennis for eight months; on September 14, Serena learns her sister, Yetunde, was shot to death in Los Angeles.

2005
In January, Serena wins the Australian Open.

2008
In September, Serena wins the U.S. Open to reclaim the top ranking in women's tennis.

2009-2010
Serena wins the Australian Open and Wimbledon in back-to-back years.

2011
Serena is named a UNICEF Goodwill Ambassador.

2012
Serena adds two more Grand Slam titles to her tally, winning Wimbledon and the U.S. Open; in July, she also wins the Olympic singles gold medal in London, and, with Venus, adds the Olympic doubles title—their third doubles gold medal.

2013
Serena wins the French Open and U.S. Open.

2014
Serena wins the U.S. Open, starting her second Serena Slam.

2015
Serena completes her second Serena Slam, winning the Australian Open, French Open, and Wimbledon; in September, she misses a calendar-year Grand Slam by losing in the semifinals of the U.S. Open; in December, she is named *Sports Illustrated*'s Sportsperson of the Year.

2016
Serena wins Wimbledon for the seventh time, tying Steffi Graf for most Open-era Grand Slam titles (22) and wins the Wimbledon doubles title with Venus, but she comes home without a medal from the Olympics.

For More Information

Books

Anniss, Matt, and Hope Killcoyne. *Venus & Serena Williams in the Community*. Chicago, IL: Britannica Educational Publishing, 2014.
Anniss and Killcoyne provide readers with a closer look at the Williams sisters' lives on and off the court, with special focus on their charitable efforts.

Rineberg, Dave. *Venus & Serena: My Seven Years as Hitting Coach for the Williams Sisters*. Hollywood, FL: Frederick Fell, 2001.
Rineberg's account of his time as the Williams sisters' hitting coach offers unique insight into their historic rise to the top of the tennis world.

Williams, Richard. *Black and White: The Way I See It*. New York, NY: Atria Books, 2014.
Richard Williams presents readers with his life story, including the highs and lows of raising and coaching two of the greatest tennis players of all time.

Williams, Serena, and Daniel Paisner. *On the Line*. Boston, MA: Grand Central, 2009.
Serena's autobiography is an intimate, entertaining look at her life through 2009 that is worthwhile reading for anyone interested in this tennis superstar.

Williams, Serena, Venus Williams, and Hilary Beard. *Venus & Serena: Serving from the Hip, 10 Rules for Living, Loving and Winning*. Boston, MA: Houghton Mifflin, 2005.
This book includes biographical material on the Williams sisters' lives, as well as their opinions and advice on a wide variety of subjects.

Williams, Serena, Venus Williams, and Russell Sadur. *How to Play Tennis: Learn How to Play Tennis with the Williams Sisters*. New York, NY: DK Publishing, 2004.
This book, which was written by the Williams sisters, provides an introduction to tennis for young people looking to begin playing the sport.

Websites

The *New York Times*: Serena Williams (www.nytimes.com/topic/person/serena-williams)
The *New York Times* has covered Serena Williams's career since its earliest days, and its vast collection of articles about her have been compiled in this archive.

Serena Williams (serenawilliams.com)
Serena's official website includes news reports, photographs, blog posts written by the tennis star, and a short biography.

Serena Williams on Instagram (www.instagram.com/serenawilliams/)
Serena's official Instagram account features photos from her personal and professional life.

Serena Williams: Player Profile (www.espn.com/tennis/player/_/id/394/serena-williams)
ESPN's Serena Williams page features stats, articles, and videos related to her career.

Serena Williams on Twitter (twitter.com/serenawilliams)
Serena uses her official Twitter account to connect with her fans through short messages and links to additional content.

73 Q's with Serena Williams (video.vogue.com/watch/serena-williams-73-questions-behind-the-scenes-clothing-launch)
This video shows Serena answering 73 questions about her life for *Vogue* magazine, giving viewers a better look at who she is away from the tennis court.

WTA (www.wtatennis.com)
The Women's Tennis Association's official website features information about Serena and Venus Williams, as well as many other female tennis stars.

Index

Picture Credits

Cover, pp. 7, 54 Leonard Zhukovsky/Shutterstock.com; p. 10 TIMOTHY A. CLARY/Staff/AFP/Getty Images; p. 11 Julian Finney/Staff/Getty Images Sport/Getty Images; pp. 12, 19, 30 Paul Harris/Contributor/Getty Images Sport/Getty Images; p. 15 Ron Chapple/Corbis/VCG/Getty Images; p. 17 D Dipasupil/Contributor/FilmMagic/Getty Images; p. 22 Ken Levine/Staff/Getty Images Sports/Getty Images; p. 26 Stephane Cardinale - Corbis/Contributor/Corbis Sport/Getty Images; p. 28 Franck Seguin/Contributor/Corbis Sport/Getty Images; p. 29 Al Bello/Staff/Getty Images Sport/Getty Images; p. 33 AP Photo/Michael S. Green; p. 35 DON EMMERT/Staff/AFP/Getty Images; p. 38 THOMAS COEX/Staff/AFP/Getty Images; p. 40 Gary Hershorn/Contributor/Corbis Sport/Getty Images; p. 41 Mark Sandten/Staff/Bongarts/Getty Images; p. 45 GERRY PENNY/Staff/AFP/Getty Images; pp. 47, 63 Cynthia Lum/Contributor/Getty Images Sport/Getty Images; p. 48 Mark Dadswell/Staff/Getty Images Sport/Getty Images; p. 51 FREDERIC J. BROWN/Staff/AFP/Getty Images; p. 55 Steve Grayson/Staff/WireImage/Getty Images; p. 56 JEAN-LOUP GAUTREAU/Staff/AFP/Getty Images; p. 59 Chris Polk/Contributor/FilmMagic/Getty Images; p. 61 Thomas Concordia/Contributor/WireImage/Getty Images; p. 65 Mike Hewitt/Staff/Getty Images Sport/Getty Images; p. 67 SIMON MAINA/Stringer/AFP/Getty Images; p. 70 ben radford/Contributor/Corbis Sport/Getty Images; p. 73 EMMANUEL DUNAND/Staff/AFP/Getty Images; p. 75 Jack Thomas/Stringer/Getty Images Sport/Getty Images; p. 78 Barcroft Media/Contributor/Barcroft Media/Getty Images; p. 81 Kyodo News/Contributor/Kyodo News/Getty Images; p. 83 Amanda Edwards/Stringer/Getty Images Entertainment/Getty Images; p. 86 Tim Clayton - Corbis/Contributor/Corbis Sport/Getty Images.

About the Author

Andrew Pina writes and edits on a freelance basis. He has written books about sports and government, and he has written and edited for websites covering football and college sports. Andrew has also edited educational, nonfiction, and reference books and materials covering music, crafts, history, science, math, and a wide array of other subject matter. Andrew has lived in the United States, France, South Korea, and Canada. In South Korea, he taught at Moonhwa High School, a college preparatory boarding school in the historic and beautiful city of Gyeongju. Andrew enjoys traveling, languages, and learning about different cultures. Today, he resides in Toronto, Ontario, Canada.